BEYOND BAPTISM

BEYOND BAPTISM

THE FIRST STEPS TOWARD HEAVEN

Kevin Rhodes

P.O. Box 3687
Cleburne, TX 76033
HopkinsPublishing.com

Copyright © 2012 Kevin W. Rhodes
www.convictionsofhonor.com
ISBN: 1-62080-996-6
ISBN-13: 978-1-62080-996-9
Library of Congress Control Number: 2012942807
Version 1.1
Cover Image: Owens Classic Image

DISCOVER OTHER TITLES
BY HOPKINS PUBLISHING
HOPKINSPUBLISHING.COM

To my two daughters,
Makaria Faith and Hannah Charis,
who have brought me such joy in life,
but never as much as when
I had the privilege of baptizing you
and calling you not only my daughters
but also my sisters in Christ.
May you ever be faithfully His,
And may you ever grow beyond baptism.

ACKNOWLEDGMENTS

The number of souls who have contributed to this volume is too great to record. Those whom I have taught over the years have all had an impact in shaping these thoughts and words. The elders at Granbury Street who first requested a class on fundamentals inspired the creation of this material and therefore deserve first mention. My wife helped with the proofreading as she had time, wrote most of the discussion questions and assignments, and used this material in its infancy in teaching others. Her suggestions along the way have improved this material immensely. Rick Popejoy has been such a great encourager over the years in bringing this material to publication, for which I thank him profusely. There are many others who have contributed in other ways, sometimes if only to send a short note of thanks that spurred me on in my writing. But ultimately my hope is that this work, as with all others, brings souls closer to their Savior and brings glory to our God.

CONTENTS

PREFACE

Just prior to His ascending to heaven, Jesus said, "All authority has been given to Me in heaven and on earth. Go therefore and make disciples of all the nations, baptizing them in the name of the Father and of the Son and of the Holy Spirit, teaching them to observe all things that I have commanded you; and lo, I am with you always, even to the end of the age" (Matt. 28:18-20). This short passage emphasizes the recognition of our Lord's authority, charges believers with the responsibility of spreading God's message of salvation to the lost throughout the world, and specifies that obeying this message by submitting to immersion is what makes a relationship with God, with Jesus, and with the Holy Spirit possible. However, the last verse contains an important exhortation as well. Those who have obeyed the gospel need ongoing instruction from more mature Christians in order to correct their misunderstandings, to encourage them in their walk, to help them adjust to the new pressures of the new life, and to develop in them a pattern of submission to Christ and His Word.

In many cases, people have been converted to baptism, but not to Christ. They have become convinced to obey the gospel's command to be immersed for the remission of sins (Acts 2:38) but have not learned completely how to surrender their will to God's revealed will. This does not mean that people must know everything about New Testament Christianity prior to their obedience, but we certainly should make sure that they understand that their baptism indicates a commitment not for a moment but for a lifetime.

Most of all, we must be as involved, as energetic, and as committed to grounding new Christians in the faith as we are to getting them into the water. After all, our goal is not to place a tally on the tote board but to see a soul reach heaven. We must never believe that a person's attendance guarantees his growth. We must remember that people have problems prior to their conversion that require attention even after their conversion. We must continue to focus on humble obedience to the Master's will, first in our own lives, and then in others' (Gal. 6:1). We must recognize that our responsibilities to a person's soul extend beyond baptism.

If you have recently become a Christian, allow me to welcome you to God's family. It is a decision you will never regret. The life of a Christian is by no means easy. In fact, Jesus Himself guarantees that there will be difficulties, but it is still the best life. I hope you know how much God loves you and how much those who have taken the time to teach you the gospel love you. Indeed, all who love the truth rejoice with you in your newfound freedom from sin.

In the pages ahead I hope to remind you of a few things you already know, answer some questions you may have been curious about, and introduce you to a few things you probably did not know. While the joy of having our sins forgiven is a wonderful feeling, we must never treat our baptism as the end of the journey, for it truly is only the beginning. Later in life, the apostle Paul said, "Brethren, I do not count myself to have apprehended; but one thing I do, forgetting those things which are behind and reaching forward to those things which are ahead, I press toward the goal for the prize of the upward call of God in Christ Jesus" (Phil. 3:13-14). When we stay on track spiritually, the Christian life is a life of constant growth, searching, learning, and applying God's will to our lives in a number of different and sometimes unexpected ways.

When you became a Christian, you made the most important decision of your life. However, I hope you realize that this decision will have meaning in eternity only if you follow up on it with the spiritual development that God wants to bring to your life. The apostle Peter reminds us that the freedom from sin and the precious promises of God are wonderful indeed, but he noted that something more was required: "But also for this very reason, giving all diligence, add to your faith virtue, to virtue knowledge, to knowledge self control, to self-control perseverance, to perseverance godliness, to godliness brotherly kindness, and to brotherly kindness love. For if these things are yours and abound, you will be neither barren nor unfruitful in the knowledge of our Lord Jesus Christ. For he who lacks these things is shortsighted, even to blindness, and has forgotten that he was cleansed from his old sins. Therefore, brethren, be even more diligent to make your call and election sure, for if you do these things you will never stumble; for so an entrance will be supplied to you abundantly into the everlasting kingdom of our Lord and Savior Jesus Christ " (2 Pet. 1:5-11). Although Peter was writing to Christians, he emphasized their need to develop their character spiritually and their lives spiritually so that they would solidify their faith, ever looking to the time when those promises can be realized in heaven itself.

This is our hope for you. In the brief studies that lie ahead, we hope to begin that process to strengthen your faith so that you might make this not simply a decision for the moment but your practice for a lifetime. So far, you have probably noticed how much emphasis people have placed on baptism—and rightly so. However, from this point forward, it will be our purpose to help you see the life that lies beyond baptism. "Or do you not know that as many of us as were baptized into Christ Jesus were baptized into His death? Therefore we were buried with Him through baptism into death, that just as Christ was raised from the dead by the glory of the Father, even so we also should walk in newness of life" (Rom. 6:3-4).

Kevin W. Rhodes

June 1, 2012

CHAPTER ONE: YOU'VE ONLY JUST BEGUN

WHERE DO I GO FROM HERE?

It is difficult to match the thrill and joy of obeying the gospel. The Ethiopian eunuch knew that joy well (Acts 8:39), and so has everyone who has called upon the name of the Lord by being immersed into Christ (Acts 22:16; Gal. 3:26-27). However, that original joy can subside rather quickly once you realize that the complete forgiveness found in that watery grave (Acts 2:38) does not ward off Satan's attacks on its own (Jas. 4:7). Temptation still lurks nearby, ever seeking to make inroads to corrupt that newly cleansed soul.

Coupled with this is the usual downturn in Bible study. At the close of Matthew's account of the gospel, he writes, "And Jesus came and spoke to them, saying, 'All authority has been given to Me in heaven and on earth. Go therefore and make disciples of all the nations, baptizing them in the name of the Father and of the Son and of the Holy Spirit, teaching them to observe all things that I have commanded you; and lo, I am with you always, even to the end of the age.' Amen" (Mt. 28:18-20). Sadly, those who provided so much attention to teaching the plan of salvation do not always follow the Lord's plan and continue in a plan of instruction following baptism. This can leave a new Christian feeling lonely, when that person should be introduced to the joys of Christian fellowship and the necessity of ongoing study and growth. Peter said, "as newborn babes, desire the pure milk of the word, that you may grow thereby" (1 Pet. 2:2), to which he later added, " but grow in the grace and knowledge of our Lord and Savior Jesus Christ" (2 Pet. 3:18a). Unfortunately, spiritual growth requires more than just attending Bible Class and Worship regularly, though these are essential (Heb. 10:24-25). For the babe in Christ to mature he or she must receive the proper nourishment. This is the responsibility of both the new Christian and the congregation.

We must admit that part of the reason a new convert may have trouble is because when that person is instructed to hear (Rom. 10:17), believe (Heb. 11:6), repent (Acts 17:30), confess (Rom. 10:9-10), and be baptized (Acts 2:38), it is often taught with a limited end in mind: baptism. But the point of teaching someone the gospel is not simply to convince them into the water but to lead them to heaven. Therefore, our plans as Christians in teaching should look toward the long-term rather than just the tallying up of baptism numbers.

But the new Christian need not feel anxious. The principles learned in order to become a child of God, if applied, will lead to spiritual growth and faithful Christian living as a child of God. We simply must be as serious about this process as we were in becoming Christians in the first place.

LISTENING TO GOD'S WORD

One of the first lessons a person must learn in order to become a Christian is to look to God's Word for spiritual answers. Many today have created barriers to their own spiritual development by assuming that spiritual insight comes from within rather than from what God has revealed. The apostle Paul wrote, "So then faith comes by hearing, and hearing by the word of God" (Rom. 10:17). But while many will refer to this verse to note the role of God's Word in producing faith, we often fail to realize that it is also our constant attention to God's Word that produces faithfulness.

God's Word should remain our source for spiritual information and instruction throughout our lives, and our response to what we find there should be as positive and enthusiastic as the first time we believed (Acts 8:35-39). Listening to God's Word must mean more than our attention to the steps of salvation. God gave His Word not only to teach us how to become Christians but also to instruct us in how to behave as Christians. Therefore, Christians must always retain an openness and eagerness to hear what God says on any and every subject, including personal behavior.

What good does it do for us to listen to God about baptism for the remission of sins (Acts 2:38) if we refuse to listen to God in regard to how we treat one another (Jn. 13:34-35; Eph. 4:32; Rom. 12:10)? What good does it do for us to listen to God when it comes to worship in spirit and truth (Jn. 4:24) if we disregard what He says about attitudes such as pride (Prov. 14:12), malice (1 Pet. 2:1), and envy (Gal. 5:21)? If we congratulate ourselves on having listened to God about some things, while ignoring others, how do we differ from the Pharisees of Jesus' day?

Jesus said, "Therefore take heed how you hear. For whoever has, to him more will be given; and whoever does not have, even what he seems to have will be taken from him" (Lk. 8:18). We must listen to God's Word with serious reflection, considering what changes we need to make to our lives. Listening to God's Word should never become a passive reaction from the pew. For the Christian it should ever remain a constant reality in everyday life.

ACCEPTING GOD'S BELIEF SYSTEM

We all have a belief system of one kind or another. Some people might describe theirs as a "worldview," but the substance remains the same. Our belief system is what determines how we look at the world, what we value, what our priorities are, and what we refuse to believe. Our belief system is the prism through which we see others and, most importantly, ourselves.

Unfortunately our society has succumbed to the doctrine of moral equivalency, so that most people have accepted the notion that all belief systems are created equal. (Of course, many in government would have you believe that secular humanism is a superior belief system.) But just because something is a "belief system" does not mean that it is above scrutiny. People believe all kinds of things, but *a belief only has real value when it is grounded in reality*. A person may not believe in gravity, but that belief has no real value. In fact, should he attempt to step off a building, the belief system will quickly be replaced by reality. Since belief systems have an ethical component to them (what is right and wrong?), they should be evaluated according to spiritual reality—truth—which has been revealed to us by God, who is spirit, in His Word (Jn. 4:24; 17:17; 1 Cor. 2:12-13).

The writer of Hebrews describes faith as "the substance of things hoped for, the evidence of things not seen" (Heb. 11:1). So faith is a matter of adopting beliefs based upon something other than our own personal experience. In order to become a Christian, we must accept the spiritual reality of our sinfulness (Rom. 3:23) as well as the spiritual reality of God's plan for our forgiveness. This is what faith is all about. We all come to the Bible with a belief system of some sort, but real faith requires us to reject our own belief system and to replace it in our hearts with God's belief system (Heb. 11:6; Rom. 1:16-17; 10:17).

REMAIN PREPARED FOR CORRECTION

"I'm sorry, so sorry." These are the lyrics to a classic song that double as a classic refrain among people from all walks of life when it comes to their sinfulness. It is amazing how hard some people find it to acknowledge that they have sinned (Lk. 15:21), but worse still is the rather pompous attitude that "I'm sorry" should be quite enough to make everything better.

Now, we should not downplay too much the major step it is for some people to admit to others that they have done something wrong. However, neither should we stop just with the admission. Paul wrote to the Corinthians, "For godly sorrow produces repentance leading to salvation, not to be regretted; but the sorrow of the world produces death. For observe this very thing, that you sorrowed in a godly manner: What diligence it produced in you, what clearing of yourselves, what indignation, what fear, what vehement desire, what zeal, what vindication! In all things you proved yourselves to be clear in this matter" (2 Cor. 7:10-11). Sorrow is a starting point for the Christian rather than an ending point.

Christians should maintain an attitude of repentance perpetually. That is, we should always be prepared to accept correction when God's Word demonstrates to us where we fall short (Jas. 1:22-25). To repent is to change your own thinking by accepting God's way of thinking. As we learn more about what God expects in our lives, we must continue to make changes in our lives.

The changes we make when we first become Christians therefore are just the beginning of this process.

OPENLY ACKNOWLEDGE THE TRUTH

Before becoming a Christian, one must make a confession, publicly stating a belief in the deity of Jesus Christ (Acts 8:36-38; Matt. 10:32-33) and full acceptance of the gospel message (Mk. 16:15-16). However, sometimes this acknowledgement gets reduced to a formula that fails to capture the full force of the biblical precept's intention.

Confession is to say the same thing, or more precisely, to acknowledge what it known to be true. So when we confess that Jesus Christ is the Son of God we should be acknowledging the identity of the historical Jesus who came to be our Savior (Matt. 1:21) as God's Anointed (Ps. 2:2) who is deity (Jn. 1:1-3; Heb. 1:1-3; Col. 1:16-17) and maintained the perfect character of deity (Heb. 4:15; 1 Pet. 2:21-22) while in the flesh (Jn. 1:14) through His submission to the Father's will (Matt. 26:39). However, we would be sadly mistaken should we assume that this is the only truth we are acknowledging. To confess the identity of Jesus Christ is also a recognition and acknowledgement that we have sinned and therefore need a Savior (Rom. 3:23), that we are responsible to our Creator (Rom. 1:25), that our way is not the right way (Jer. 10:23), and that we acknowledge that only our submission to God's will can remedy our situation (Rom. 12:1-2; Heb. 5:8-9). Confession is no small step.

We must realize that confession is not limited to one time or to one doctrine of the Bible. As Christians we should be prepared to openly acknowledge God's truth anywhere and everywhere, before anyone and everyone (1 Pet. 3:15). God is right; we are wrong. This is true not about one thing but about all things. And the only way we become right is by accepting the way of God, who is right.

OBEY GOD

Most religious people agree that you should obey God. The problem is that most people also want to amend this agreement to obey by attaching various exception clauses. They will argue that obedience is the right thing to do but not a required thing to do, apparently failing to realize that such a position means that they believe doing what is right is not really required. In other words, they want to treat the New Testament as if it were Chicken Soup for the Soul.

The writer to the Hebrews recalls of Jesus that, "though He was a Son, yet He learned obedience by the things which He suffered. And having been perfected, He became the author of eternal salvation to all who obey Him" (Heb. 5:8-9). God required obedience of Jesus, despite the close relationship they shared. Jesus' perfect obedience made it possible for Him to provide salvation to those who are imperfect, but this still depends upon their obedience to His will (Jn. 12:48; Lk. 6:46; Mt. 7:21-23).

Peter preached immersion in water for the remission of sins on the Day of Pentecost (Acts 2:38), as did those who followed (Acts 22:16), and as we must today. But baptism is just the beginning. It initiates our renewed relationship with God through Jesus Christ (Gal. 3:26-27) by demonstrating our willingness to submit our will to God's will. Baptism begins our new spiritual life because of our obedience (Rom. 6:3-4), but it is our ongoing obedience to God that sustains that new life. "Little children, let no one deceive you. He who practices righteousness is righteous, just as He is righteous" (1 Jn. 3:7).

THE FIRST STEPS IN A NEW WALK

New Christians often have a hard time adjusting to their new life. Part of this is due to the natural difficulties associated with making life-altering changes, but part of this is due to our collective failure as teachers to provide ongoing instruction after baptism. Should we really be surprised when Christians treat baptism as the end when we as their spiritual guides imply as much?

While a new Christian has much to learn about the Bible, the church, studying, and Christian living, he or she can take heart that the same principles that made salvation and this new life possible also form the basis for a new Christian to continue his or her growth. The common refrain of "Hear, Believe, Repent, Confess, and Be Baptized" may apply only to the non-Christian, but the underlying principles go hand in hand with Christian living. A Christian goes to God's Word as the authoritative source of spiritual information (Rom. 4:3), accepts what God says and makes any adjustments to personal beliefs that are necessary (Heb. 5:12-14), determines to correct those things in his or her life that are out of line with what the Bible says (Acts 8:22), maintains a willingness to speak up about God's Will and acknowledge wrongdoing (1 Pet. 3:15; 1 Jn. 1:9), and seeks to obey God in all things, whether by the elimination of what is wrong or the introduction of what is right (Heb. 5:8-9).

Paul said, "Or do you not know that as many of us as were baptized into Christ Jesus were baptized into His death? Therefore we were buried with Him through baptism into death, that just as Christ was raised from the dead by the glory of the Father, even so we also should walk in newness of life" (Rom. 6:3-4). Baptism is essential, but it is just the beginning.

DISCUSSION QUESTIONS:

1. Look at the boldface headings for each section in this lesson. What is another way to word these captions (hint: it would be what we normally refer to as "the plan of salvation")?

2. Are the "five steps of salvation" one time acts or principles that a faithful Christian must follow for the rest of his or her life?

3. Do you feel you are receiving the attention you need to help you adjust to (or grow in) your life in Christ? Why or Why not?

4. When is it hardest for you to listen to God's Word?

5. What are some differences—if any—in a Christian's worldview and the world's attitude toward life?

6. Why is it so hard to accept criticism and spiritual correction? What can we do to make it easier on ourselves to admit when we are wrong?

7. If you were to have an opportunity to explain what the Bible teaches about salvation to people at school or at work, would you have trouble doing it? What do you need to do to prepare for such a situation?

8. When are we most tempted to wish obedience were not required?

9. What is the hardest thing you are going to have to adjust to as a Christian?

10. Did you learn or find out anything helpful from studying this lesson? If so, what was it?

ASSIGNMENT:

Pick one person you know who is not a Christian. Take the time this next week to tell that person about your decision to become a child of God and what brought you to that point. Then write down his or her reaction, whether positive or negative, so we can discuss it at our next study.

CHAPTER TWO:
TREATING JESUS AS LORD

Great is the number of people who claim Jesus as their Lord. Even some of the most immoral in society will verbally acknowledge the Lordship of Jesus in some manner. Such obvious inconsistency often floors us. How, we ask, can people confess Jesus as Lord in one breath while sinning in the next (Jas. 3:9-11)?

Somehow we have created distinctions between what we are willing to acknowledge verbally and what we are willing to acknowledge behaviorally. On the Day of Pentecost Peter said, "Therefore let all the house of Israel know assuredly that God has made this Jesus, whom you crucified, both Lord and Christ" (Acts 2:36). But to some "Lord" is simply a title with little real meaning. In fact, it is the lack of meaning that people attach to it that allows them to use it vainly as an exclamation (Ex. 20:7).

Regarding this very hypocrisy, Jesus asked, "But why do you call Me 'Lord, Lord,' and not do the things which I say?" (Lk. 6:46). Therefore, obedience is the true acknowledgement of Christ's Lordship (Heb. 5:8-9). We may call Jesus "Lord," but if it is not accompanied by obedience, our sincerity is dubious at best. If we are to claim Jesus as Lord, we must treat Jesus as Lord, which means we respect and submit to His authority in all things. We are servants. We do not try to bargain with our Lord. We cannot ignore something He has said. We do not put His Word up for a vote or run His authority through a committee. Jesus is Lord. Of this there is no doubt. But we must do more than call Him Lord. We must accept Him as Lord. But to accept Him as Lord requires that we treat Him as Lord.

THE SOURCE OF AUTHORITY

While some are willing to acknowledge the Lordship of Jesus Christ, including its implications regarding His authority to rule every aspect of our lives, many of these same people dispute the means by which that authority has been conveyed to mankind. Some apparently believe that divine authority is so ethereal that God could not express it. Jesus, on the other hand, said, "Not everyone who says to Me, 'Lord, Lord,' shall enter the kingdom of heaven, but he who does the will of My Father in heaven" (Mt. 7:21). This implies that God's will has been expressed, that it can be known accurately, and that it can be obeyed correctly.

Jesus promised to make the truth, which is the fullness of God's will, known (Jn. 8:32) by the inspiration of the Holy Spirit (Jn. 14:26; 15:26; 16:13). This He did through the apostles and prophets (Acts 1:2; 2 Pet. 1:19-21), so that now we have that truth fully in written form (2 Tim. 3:16-17; Jn. 17:17). Inasmuch as we have the complete word of God (2 Pet. 1:3), then we also can know the complete will of God according to which we must live (Rom. 12:2; Eph. 5:17).

Respect for the authority of our Lord Jesus Christ must include respect for the word through which that authoritative message greets mankind (Jn. 12:48). Some attempt to distort this inherent connection between the authority of Christ and the authority of His Word, but Jesus, foreseeing this, has answered them already: "Many will say to Me in that day, '"Lord, Lord, have we not prophesied in Your name, cast out demons in Your name, and done many wonders in Your name?' And then I will declare to them, "I never knew you; depart from Me, you who practice lawlessness!"'" (Mt. 7:22-23).

THE WORDS OF AUTHORITY

Words matter. As one radio talk-show host says, "Words mean things." Words communicate. Divine words matter more, mean more, and communicate more. Jesus said, "And if anyone hears My words and does not believe, I do not judge him; for I did not come to judge the world but to save the world. He who rejects Me, and does not receive My words, has that which judges him—the word that I have spoken will judge him in the last day" (Jn. 12:47-48).

From the way some people talk about the Bible, you would think that words are meaningless. They want to talk about Jesus, but not mention what He said. They want to talk about doctrine, but not discuss the words by which we come to know doctrine (2 Tim. 3:16-17). Words matter. Notice what Jesus said. Divine words carry the message that makes eternal life possible (Jn. 12:50). While Jesus did not come the first time for the purpose of judgment, He did come to leave the standard of judgment. The Divine Word is the collection and connection of Divine words. The Word (logos) is authoritative because all of the words (rhemata) were spoken with authority.

To reject "He who believes and is baptized will be saved" (Mk. 16:16a) is to reject Christ. To not accept that "God is spirit, and those who worship Him must worship in spirit and truth" (Jn. 4:24) is to not accept Jesus. The statements of the Bible spoken with Divine authority carry Divine authority and will be the standard against which we are judged—by Divine authority. Our God included all of these words in the text for a reason: they matter. Therefore, as we study and learn we must accept them without fail through our obedience to show that these words matter to us.

THE PATTERN OF AUTHORITY

When the Lord gave instruction to Moses regarding the tabernacle and its furniture, He told Him, "And see to it that you make them according to the pattern which was shown you on the mountain" (Ex. 25:40). Furthermore, the writer of Hebrews quoted this passage to show that even this pattern was only a shadow for a greater pattern in Christianity (Heb. 8:5). However, some people today reject the entire concept of a biblical pattern, despite the consistency with which this concept appears in the Scriptures.

A pattern indicates an example to be followed. Paul offered himself as an example (1 Tim. 1:16) based on Christ's example (1 Cor. 11:1) and told Titus to instruct the younger men to live so that their lives could be a pattern for others as well. Therefore, a spiritual pattern is one that indicates behavior that pleases God that is set forth as a whole. While people rarely have trouble accepting the idea of a personal pattern for Christianity, they often stumble over the pattern for church behavior, yet the principle is the same for both. When a congregation's actions are recorded with divine approval in Holy Writ, then those behaviors form the foundation for our understanding of what God approves of as proper, acceptable congregational behavior. When all of these actions are put together, they form a pattern for the church (Mt. 16:18-19; Eph. 5:25-27).

Determining which actions of the early church constitute a pattern may not always be simple, but there should be no dispute that there is a pattern. The examples provided in the New Testament regarding the church are there for our benefit. If a church rejects "pattern theology" then you know that they are not a good "example" of the New Testament church.

THE IMPLICATIONS OF AUTHORITY

The Jews of the first century trusted in their heritage greatly, especially when it came to being descendants of Abraham. To them, this freed them from all burdens. When Jesus told them they needed the truth, they replied, "We are Abraham's descendants" (Jn. 8:33). To them, no one could be greater than Abraham. Jesus, on the other hand, told them that they had no claim to righteousness on the basis of their lineage because they would not listen to a message from God (Jn. 8:47), which Abraham was willing to do.

These Jews became even more furious when Jesus told them, " if anyone keeps My word he shall never see death" (Jn. 8:51). To them this was blasphemy, because this meant that Jesus was claiming to be greater than Abraham, who had himself died (Jn. 8:52). Therefore, they asked Jesus, "Who do you make yourself out to be?" (Jn. 8:53). The Jews had assumed a posture of self-righteousness based upon their relationship to Abraham, but Jesus argued that Abraham was not on their side but on His: "Your father Abraham rejoiced to see my day, and he saw it and was glad" (Jn. 8:56). But the Jews quickly countered by arguing that for such a statement to be true then Jesus would have to have seen Abraham, which to them His appearance ruled out immediately (Jn. 8:57).

Jesus then said, "Most assuredly, I say to you, before Abraham was, I am" (Jn. 8:58). Using a contrast in verbs, the present tense, and an allusion to Exodus 3:14, Jesus answered the question of how He knew Abraham and the question regarding His identity they had posed earlier.

They did not like the answer (Jn. 8:59), but they understood it. And that is the point. This whole discussion depended upon both Jesus and the Jews using implication in what they said and inferring what the other had implied. Jesus expected the Jews to understand the implications of His words; in fact, His words required that they do so. He requires the same of us: to think and to reason about what the words say and what the words imply (Isa. 1:17-18).

THE ACCEPTANCE OF AUTHORITY

After Jesus fed the five thousand, people followed after Him. However, they did not follow because they recognized Jesus to be the Messiah, or even a prophet. They followed Him because they wanted another free meal (Jn. 6:26-31). Instead of bowing to their wishes, Jesus told them that they had a greater need than physical hunger; they needed spiritual life, which could only come from Him—the bread of life (Jn. 6:32-35)—and their acceptance of the message He brought from God (Jn. 6:36-40).

The Jews rejected the message because they rejected Jesus as the Messenger. But Jesus reiterated the necessity of accepting His message as divinely authoritative in order to have spiritual life (Jn. 6:41-51). Moreover, He then told them that nothing short of complete acceptance of His authority (eating His flesh and drinking His blood) was acceptable in order to be His disciple and enjoy the promise of the resurrection and eternal life (Jn. 6:52-59).

"Many therefore of his disciples, when they had heard this, said, This is a hard saying; who can hear it?" (Jn. 6:60 KJV), to which Jesus asked, "Does this offend you?" (Jn. 6:61). To them, His asking for complete obedience was too much, and so, "From that time many of his disciples went back and walked with him no more" (Jn. 6:66). Their commitment to Jesus was incomplete because their acceptance of His authority was incomplete. But no matter how many people rejected Him, what He said was still true. "Then Jesus said to the twelve, "Do you also want to go away?" But Simon Peter answered Him, "Lord, to whom shall we go? You have the words of eternal life. Also we have come to believe and know that You are the Christ, the Son of the living God" (Jn. 6:67-69). The complete authority of Jesus Christ and the truth of the gospel does not depend upon our acceptance of His authority—our salvation does (Mt. 7:23; Jn. 8:32; 17:17; Acts 4:12; Col. 3:17)!

DISCUSSION QUESTIONS:

Please list at least one scripture reference that you used to answer each question.

1. Why is simply <u>claiming</u> Jesus as Lord not enough to make a right relationship with Him?

2. Taking the Lord's name in vain demonstrates what underlying attitude?

3. Can God's will really be understood by mere human beings?

4. Can we respect Jesus without respecting (and therefore obeying) His words from the Bible? Why or why not?

5. When trying to understand how the Bible authorizes (or gives permission), we must truly believe that all its words are inspired of God. Why does this matter today?

6. In what three ways does the Bible authorize? Please give an example of each.

7. Just how much of Jesus' authority must people accept today?

8. Why is it dangerous to "pick and choose" which of God's commands we will follow when determining how we will live?

9. What parts of the New Testament do you find difficult to accept?

10. What did you learn from studying this lesson?

ASSIGNMENT:

Make a list of the three biggest problems in your life right now. Once that is completed, ask another Christian to help you find what God says in the scriptures about handling those problems. Finally, decide what might be the most difficult part to accept for each problem in order to please God.

What will you do now to make sure that you will treat Jesus as Lord even in these bigger problems of life?

CHAPTER THREE: RESPECTING INSPIRATION

The apostle Paul told Timothy, "All Scripture is given by inspiration of God, and is profitable for doctrine, for reproof, for correction, for instruction in righteousness, that the man of God may be complete, thoroughly equipped for every good work" (2 Tim. 3:16-17). We have the opportunity to pick up a Bible whenever and wherever we wish. But do we really understand and appreciate what it is we are holding?

Anything that we are going to respect and treat with spiritual authority must come from God. While the English word "inspiration" refers to what was "breathed in," the Greek word theopneustos refers to what is breathed out. Therefore, Paul emphasized not the men who received the message but the God who gave it. The apostle Peter wrote, " for prophecy never came by the will of man, but holy men of God spoke as they were moved by the Holy Spirit" (2 Pet. 1:21). The origin of the Bible is divine, and the guidance in writing the Bible was divine. Thus, though the Bible was penned by human writers who brought their experiences and personality to the page, because both author and editor were divine, making the process divine, insuring that the final result was, and is, divine, this message carries God's authority.

We as Christians must respect inspiration. The Bible is not just inspiring and motivational, the Bible is not just inspiring in its quality and beauty; the Bible is inspired by God. It is our understanding and appreciation for the divine origin of this message and these words that will cause us to respect this message and these words. We cannot take God's message "with a grain of salt." We must receive the gospel for what it is: God's personal message for all mankind (1 Th. 2:13).

RESPECT EVERY WORD

Many religious people claim to believe in and respect the inspiration of the scriptures; however, their definitions of inspiration reveal a lack of confidence in God's Book and their embarrassment concerning some portions of scripture. A growing number of Christians are actively promoting the idea of "thought inspiration," a concept which attempts to honor God as the original source of "salvational and doctrinal" matters recorded in the Bible while suggesting that other information (scientific, historical, etc.) comes solely from the men who wrote it. Such a view compromises the integrity of scripture inherently as well as contradicting the Bible's own claims regarding its origin and extent of inspiration.

According to Jesus, we will be judged according to the "words" of "the word" (Jn. 12:48). Paul also described the process of inspiration in his first epistle to the Corinthians as the deliverance of "words" to speak (1 Cor. 2:12-13), just as Jesus had promised the apostles that it would be given to them what to "say" (Mt. 10:19). Furthermore, Paul said, "For what does the scripture say?" (Rom. 4:3) as an authoritative appeal—not an authoritative idea, but an authoritative selection of specific words.

Those who compromise regarding the integrity of scripture, who want to bow down before the gods of secular pseudo-scholars, probably do not realize the implications of their capitulation. As Moses prepared the Israelites to continue to follow God after his own death, He said, "Set your hearts on all the words which I testify among you today, which you shall command your children to be careful to observe—all the words of this law" (Deut. 32:46). So too must we today show respect not only for the doctrines of the Bible but also for every single inspired word.

RESPECT WHAT GOD SAYS

You would probably be amazed at the number of people who claim to believe the Bible. However, this actually translates into believing something about the Bible or believing some of the things in the Bible. Even in the church there are those who place limitations upon what they will accept on the pages of Holy Writ. Modernists have made such inroads into society and into the scholar's psyche that well-meaning brethren sometimes allow their faith in scholarship to supercede their faith in God's Word (Rom. 10:17; 2 Tim. 3:16).

To respect what God says demands that we respect ALL that God says, whether it is doctrinal, psychological, historical, or scientific. This does not mean that we should attempt to force a 21st century construct onto the Bible. The Bible does not have to mention "genus" and "species" to be correct scientifically in its references to different "kinds." Even an evolutionist refers to a "sunset," despite his understanding that the earth revolves around the sun. It is not necessary for the Bible always to employ a chronological approach to be correct in its history. (This is even rare in secular history today.) Most of the alleged contradictions people cite are simply different perspectives or people using a difference frame of reference. If one person says he watched a TV show in its original broadcast at 9 pm while another makes the same claim for 8 pm, is it not possible that they are both correct, each living in a different time zone?

The Bible is not a science textbook, but it is accurate in its scientific information. The Bible is not a history text, but its history is completely accurate. Those who have so little confidence in the Bible's accuracy and integrity should talk a lot less about the Bible and study it a lot more (2 Tim. 2:15; Rom. 1:16).

RESPECT WHAT GOD DOES NOT SAY

The fact of verbal plenary inspiration makes anything God does NOT say significant because it is not due to oversight or lack of attention. When God does not include something in His Word or give approval to something in His Covenant, it is because He does not want it there and because He does not approve of it.

In Deuteronomy 29:29 Moses wrote, "The secret things belong to the LORD our God, but those things which are revealed belong to us and to our children forever, that we may do all the words of this law." More than likely, many have heard references to these "secret things," but rarely in their context, which is that of revelation. In other words, Moses told the people, "Do not even bother speculating about what God has not told you. You make sure you are doing what He HAS told you to do." (In fact, these "secret things" of Moses correlate to what Paul calls the "mystery," which God made known in the gospel (Eph. 1:9, etc.)). In Acts 15:24 certain men were condemned for going beyond what had been revealed. In Hebrews 7:14 the writer argues that the Messiah could not be a priest under the law of Moses because it said nothing about priesthood concerning the tribe of Judah.

The division in the religious world exists primarily due to the lack of respect for God's silence and the resulting differences caused by their subsequent speculation beyond what God has revealed. Paul told the Galatians to reject a message that made ANY alteration to the gospel—including addition or subtraction—because those changes, however small, meant that the message was no longer truly the gospel because its changed message was no longer from God (Gal. 1:6-9).

DISCUSSION QUESTIONS:

Please give at least one applicable scripture reference when answering each question.

1. What <u>should</u> we mean when we say that the Bible is "inspired"?

2. How did the men who penned (wrote out) the books of the Bible affect its meaning? Did they have any affect at all? What evidence do you have for your answer?

3. What are the differences between "thought inspiration" and "verbal plenary inspiration"?

4. Can we respect the authority of Scripture while leaving out certain words or certain verses of the Bible?

5. Can you give some examples of teachings or practices of people in the world that demonstrate they do not really respect the inspiration of the Bible?

6. Can you give some examples of teachings or practices of members of the church that demonstrate they do not really respect the inspiration of the Bible?

7. Have you heard of any alleged "contradictions" in the Bible? Do these cause you to doubt the inspiration of God's Word? Why or why not?

8. Why do you think people seem to enjoy speculating about the things that God has not included in the Bible? What very important lessons are they usually missing when they do this?

9. What is the significance of God's silence on a matter? How does this affect the life of a Christian today?

10. What have you learned from studying this lesson?

ASSIGNMENT:

Take up the challenge, beginning today, of reading at least one chapter of God's Word every day. Ask the preacher, an elder, or a Christian friend what book might teach the most about a topic you still have trouble accepting. Then, as you read each day, think about what God has done and why His way is always best.

CHAPTER FOUR:
WHAT MAKES THE CHURCH THE CHURCH?

Peter's confession, "You are the Christ, the Son of the living God," recorded in Matthew 16:16 acknowledged several essential things: (1) that there is only one God, (2) that Jesus is the Messiah, God's anointed, and therefore the fulfillment of all of God's promises, and (3) that Jesus is of divine character. If any one of these things is untrue, then the church is meaningless. Therefore, any church that rejects any of these principles cannot be the true church because Jesus said, "on this rock I will build My church" (Matt. 16:18), which also implies that there is but one true church (Eph. 4:4-6) which will be the abode of the saved (Eph. 5:25; Acts 20:28).

Jesus' next statement continues to shed light on the nature of His church. "And I will give you the keys of the kingdom of heaven" (Matt. 16:18a). Since Jesus here treats the church and the kingdom synonymously, then any church that is waiting for a future kingdom must not be the true church (Mk. 9:1; Col. 1:13-14). But since the church is Christ's kingdom, then He is the King, which means that He holds all the authority for entrance into the kingdom, so that if one rejects Jesus' way into the church, then he is not saved (Acts 2:38,

47). Furthermore, the true church accepts without question the authority of our Lord. In His exhortation to Peter, "and whatever you bind on earth will be bound in heaven, and whatever you loose on earth will be loosed in heaven" (Matt. 16:19b), Jesus was not giving Peter or any other man authority to dictate doctrine or salvation. Just the opposite. He was telling Peter that he had the responsibility to abide by the doctrine and message of salvation written in heaven (Gal. 1:6-9).

Therefore, for a church to be the church, it must acknowledge the true identity of Jesus, respect the singularity of the church and its place as Christ's kingdom, follow the plan of entrance laid out by Jesus Himself, and remain within the doctrinal limits of the gospel, respecting it as the only means of establishing authority and the only way of knowing God's will completely.

THE CHARACTER OF THE CHURCH

What constitutes the true church? Protestants argue that all the various denominations considered as a whole make up the universal church. However, Paul taught against such division (1 Cor. 1:10) and did not allow for such doctrinal variety (Gal. 1:6-9). This concept of the church falls far short of that for which Jesus prayed (Jn. 17:21-23) and therefore is totally unacceptable to anyone who is seeking to belong to the glorious body of Christ.

There are several religious bodies that claim to be the one true church. But, as with Jesus' Lordship, making the claim is not good enough (Mt. 7:21-23). Since there can be only one true church, then the fact that many make the claim proves that the claim alone proves nothing. Some have argued that they can trace their historical heritage back to the first century. Since all churches claiming allegiance to Christ—other than the true church—either broke off from or altered the original, or broke off from or altered one of these splinter groups, then all can claim some historical tie to the true church. However, once again, that history and tradition are not sufficient. After all, if this is the basis, which splinter group is the correct splinter group? And which should be considered the splinter? Also, contrary to popular opinion, the name on the sign outside of a building does not necessarily reflect the reality of that church. There are denominations that have scriptural names, but having a scriptural name alone does not make a church scriptural. In the same manner, having

"Church of Christ" (Rom. 16:16) on a sign does not necessarily equate to that congregation being the New Testament Church.

The true church cannot be identified based upon claims, names, or historical ties. The true New Testament church can only be identified by its spiritual character.. This, in turn, can only be identified by its consistency--not with tradition, but with what the New Testament actually says (Rom. 1:16).

THE APPEAL OF THE CHURCH

Most people believe that the church they attend should be appealing. Unfortunately, most of these people think the church should be appealing to them. But this is not what the Bible teaches. Paul wrote "To the church of God which is at Corinth, to those who are sanctified in Christ Jesus, called to be saints, with all who in every place call on the name of Jesus Christ our Lord, both theirs and ours" (1 Cor. 1:2).

Paul described the church as those who "call on the name of Jesus Christ our Lord," but what does this mean? The word translated "call on" is the same word Paul used when he appealed to Caesar (Acts 25:11). Therefore, Paul described the church as people who have accepted Divine authority as the basis for all that they do and accept only appeals to Divine authority as a sure foundation on which to base action and doctrine (1 Cor. 3:11; Acts 4:12). Therefore, religions that appeal to their own developed traditions to support their behavior cannot be the body of Christ (Mt. 15:8-9). Churches that show little concern for establishing Divine approval of their activities do not belong to Jesus. Those who require texts, books, and manuals besides the Bible in order to support their doctrines do not have a Divine mandate even to exist. The Bible is sufficient (2 Tim. 3:16-17).

Should the church, as God designed it, appeal to men? Yes and No. The church should not structure its activities or doctrines in such a way as to please men (Gal. 1:10), despite the growing "community church" movement. But men who love God, love truth, and love their souls will find God's design for the church as revealed in the New Testament very appealing. For the church to be the true church, what it teaches and practices must appeal to God (Heb. 13:15-16).

THE SALVATION OF THE CHURCH

Modern myths perpetuated among many religious people insist that the church is irrelevant in matters pertaining to salvation. However, just a few verses of scripture should show how wrong such a view is and how damaging it can be. First, those in the church are identical with those who are saved (Acts 2:47). This is true because Jesus purchased the church with His blood (Acts 20:28), gave Himself for the church (Eph. 5:25), and is the Savior of the church (Eph. 5:23). Therefore, there is no salvation outside of the church, and any church to which you adjoin yourself separate and apart from your salvation cannot be Christ's church.

The "church" is a designation of all those people who have responded to God's message in faith (Rom. 10:17; Heb. 11:6) and have come together as one based upon their mutual profession of faith and submission to God's will (Acts 17:30; Rom. 10:9-10; Heb. 5:8-9) in order to obtain forgiveness and salvation, both of which are made possible only by immersion in water based upon faith in Christ (Acts 2:38; Mk. 16:16). Since entrance into the church occurs concurrently with one's salvation, it should not surprise anyone that one enters the Lord's church by immersion (1 Cor. 12:13).

Since the church (the called out, ekklesia) is identified according to people's response to the call of the gospel, then to belong to Christ's church everyone had to respond to the same call the same way—God's call and God's way. There can be only one plan of salvation, just as there can be only one true church (Eph. 4:4-6). If you want to go to heaven, you must follow that plan—God's plan (Rom. 1:16-17)—and belong to that church—Christ's church (Matt. 16:18).

THE WORSHIP OF THE CHURCH

The desire to worship seems innate in man. Most automatically recognize that there is something bigger than themselves to which they owe their existence and to which they should show obeisance. But neither this desire to worship nor the blind expression of that desire is enough on its own to please the God who deserves this worship. For God to accept our worship we must offer Him true worship, worship He requests in the manner He requests.

When Cain and Abel made offerings of worship, they both set out to worship the one true God. Therefore, the object and intent of their worship was not at issue. Yet the Lord accepted Abel's offering while rejecting Cain's (Gen. 4:4-5). According to modern theology's emphasis on sincerity and doctrinal flexibility, Jehovah God was the One who was wrong! This simply cannot be (1 Jn. 1:5; Jas. 1:13). Therefore, we must understand why Cain was wrong in his offering. He worshipped, but it was not true worship. His worship was unacceptable because it was not what God wanted. He offered something other than what God requested. The writer of Hebrews says that Abel offered his sacrifice by faith (Heb. 11:4), which means that his actions corresponded to what God had told him (Rom. 10:17; 14:23). Cain's offering of worship was unacceptable and in vain because it was not in accordance with what God told him. Cain may have had a talent for farming (Gen. 4:1), but that did not make his sacrifice acceptable. Offering the fruit of the ground may have been more pleasing to Cain, but it was totally unacceptable to God.

True worship expresses in action and devotion what God has expressed in His Word—nothing more, and nothing less. "God is spirit, and those who worship Him must worship in spirit and truth" (Jn. 4:24).

THE PEOPLE OF THE CHURCH

Immediately after obeying the gospel, most people are energetic, enthusiastic, and ready to get involved. Unfortunately, the congregation is not always energetic, enthusiastic, and ready to help people get involved, which makes it even harder on new Christians. Beyond this, many people seem to equate congregational activity with their personal Christian activity. That is, they tend to limit their involvement in divinely mandated activities to what everyone else is doing too. This is truly unfortunate because not only is this an improper view of a Christian's responsibilities, it also inhibits greater growth and activity on the part of individuals.

A Christian has responsibilities that extend beyond those involving the congregation. In fact, a congregation's activities should be, in some ways, an extension of the combination of the activities of individual Christians. First, every Christian should begin with the determination to demonstrate Christian character. Jesus went about "doing good" (Acts 10:38). This does not mean that

He worked with various charitable organizations; it means that in His daily interaction with people, He treated people with kindness, generosity, and love (Gal. 6:10). Second, our Lord has also given Christians the responsibility of introducing the gospel message to those who are lost (Mk. 16:15-16). Yes, people may have a Bible. Yes, preachers preach. But individual Christians should be the first to initiate spiritual conversation that will lead a person to the truth. Finally, every Christian should do his best to help other Christians grow in their faith (Eph. 4:16; 1 Cor. 14:26). This involves instruction and correction, often done informally (1 Th. 5:14; Gal. 6:1; Jas. 5:19-20).

God has called upon Christians to do good for others so that they might see God's goodness. He calls upon Christians to spread the good news so that those who are lost might obey and be saved. He calls upon Christians to strengthen one another so that no one falls away (Gal. 5:4) and so that there might be a united front against sin and error (Jn. 17:21). This is not what we do on Sunday; it is what we should do every day (Eph. 4:1).

THE ORGANIZATION OF THE CHURCH

When the prophet and judge Samuel grew old, his sons acted as judges for Israel. Unfortunately, they did not have the same character as Samuel. In response to this problem, the leaders of Israel called for Samuel "and said to him, "Look, you are old, and your sons do not walk in your ways. Now make us a king to judge us like all the nations" (1 Sam. 8:5). These men had recognized the problem, but they looked in the wrong place for the solution. "And the LORD said to Samuel, 'Heed the voice of the people in all that they say to you; for they have not rejected you, but they have rejected Me, that I should not reign over them'" (1 Sam. 8:7). When the church began having some difficulties in the early second century, they followed a similar pattern, and so they adopted a hierarchy in church government patterned after the Roman Empire. But this was not of God's desire or design. It was man's.

In the true church, there is no president, there is no board, and there is no individual who has control over other individuals. In the true church, every member is directly responsible to God and the Lord Jesus Christ. As Peter said, "We ought to obey God rather than men" (Acts 5:29). However, that does not mean there is no leadership within the church. Paul noted the existence of "bishops and deacons" in a local congregation (Phil. 1:1). Both of these are spiritual roles of service on behalf of the congregation. Deacons are special servants given special responsibilities that require special character (1 Tim. 3:8-12). Bishops, who are also called elders and shepherds (Acts 20:17-28), oversee the congregation and lead it spiritually by pointing people to God's Word by determining within the confines of God's will what is the most expedient way for the congregation to implement God's will.

Elders, deacons, and preachers have no authority to legislate behavior; they exist in order to help you implement divinely legislated behavior. The church is not a democracy; it is a kingdom (Mt. 16:18-19). Jesus is our king, and we are all servants. Therefore, congregational leadership is based on those who have a proven record of spiritual service (Mk. 10:42-45).

THE UNITY OF THE CHURCH

God desires unity among His people. This is undeniable. Paul told the Corinthians, "Now I plead with you, brethren, by the name of our Lord Jesus Christ, that you all speak the same thing, and that there be no divisions among you, but that you be perfectly joined together in the same mind and in the same judgment" (1 Cor. 1:10). Jesus Himself prayed, "that they all may be one, as You, Father, are in Me, and I in You; that they also may be one in Us, that the world may believe that You sent Me" (Jn. 17:21). God expects and requires unity among His people. But how do we achieve it?

Many men have attempted to bring about religious unity. Prior to the Protestant Reformation there was unity of a sort, but it was a mandated unity dictated by an organizational hierarchy. Denominationalism claims unity through interaction, yet this is very limited and superficial considering the doctrinal differences that span various protestant organizations. It is a unity achieved by temporarily setting aside differences to concentrate on a few matters of agreement. Thus, interdenominational efforts may be somewhat cooperative, but they are not unity. Non-denominationalism, which has given rise to the community church movement, recognized this weakness and encouraged people to set aside these differences permanently in order to have unity. However, this necessarily entails the rejection of instruction on any matter with which there is disagreement, or unity fails. Therefore, one cannot proclaim the whole counsel of God (Acts 20:26-27) as God requires, making non-denominationalism itself unbiblical, which means that it cannot produce unity that pleases God.

If we are to please God, we must seek unity God's way. We must set aside all doctrines and practices that separate us and begin anew by adopting only those doctrines and practices found on the pages of the New Covenant (Eph. 2:14-16). Jesus did not pray for a hodge-podge type of unity; He prayed that the church would have unity in the same manner as the Godhead. This unity can be achieved only by following what God Himself has revealed—precisely and completely.

DISCUSSION QUESTIONS:

Please give at least one applicable scripture reference when answering each question.

1. In your own words, please explain what makes the church THE church.

2. Can you identify the true church solely by the name on the outside of the church building? Conversely, does the name on the building really matter at all to God?

3. What does it mean to "call on the name of Jesus Christ our Lord" (1 Cor. 1:2)?

4. Can you be saved without being part of the church for which Christ died? What does this imply in terms of your daily life and activities?

5. Are there any circumstances where it would be possible to worship and work completely independently of a local church (i.e. you do it all on your own) and still remain pleasing to God? How do you know your answer is correct?

6. Is it enough for the congregation where you attend to be actively working for the Lord? What personal responsibilities do you have as a Christian?

7. Is it OK for religious people to just "agree to disagree" about their differences?

8. How does God want the leadership in His church to be organized? Does scripture describe these leaders as dictatorial and absolute in their "power"? How are they to properly lead the congregation?

9. What is the only way to have real unity? Have you ever seen this type of unity demonstrated?

10. What have you learned from studying this lesson?

ASSIGNMENT:

What do you see in your home congregation when it comes to being the true church we read about in the New Testament? Does it match up with what you find in the Bible? How should you respond if you find areas that do not agree with God's inspired plan for His church?

Write down any questions you have about your congregation following the Bible and ask one of the elders or the preacher to explain to you, using the scriptures, how the practice in question matches God's Word.

CHAPTER FIVE: WE SHALL ASSEMBLE

The assembly of the Lord's church is something special. It is the time that we focus on God and His Word and contemplate all that this means for us in our relationship with Deity and our relationship with one another. It is a time of praise and true fellowship, yet some have difficulties seeing this because the world has turned their assemblies into entertainment, and sometimes Christians do not even appreciate what it means to gather together.

Worship is the most fundamental expression of our relationship with God. Worship demonstrates the extent of our reverence. Worship displays the extent of our humility. Worship reveals the heart's adoration. Worship shows the world what and whom we value above all else and all others. In His discussion of worship with the woman at the well, Jesus said, "But the hour is coming, and now is, when the true worshipers will worship the Father in spirit and truth; for the Father is seeking such to worship Him. God is Spirit, and those who worship Him must worship in spirit and truth" (Jn. 4:23-24). It is not enough to worship. It is not even enough to worship Jehovah. To be a true worshiper, one must worship in spirit and truth. Therefore, what you do in worship and as worship must appeal to the spiritual nature of God, must be in accordance with divinely revealed truth (Jn. 17:17), and must seek to please God (Gal. 1:10) or it is not true worship.

Worship is the act of reverently bowing down in soul and spirit before One who is greater in order to acknowledge His superiority. But if in our worship we place our own desires above God's, how can we then claim to recognize His sovereignty? By doing so, we have placed our own will above His in priority. "Contemporary worship styles" are now all the rage, appealing to the tastes of a younger generation. But in many denominations, what people call traditional worship fulfilled the same purpose for a different generation. Many a person cannot imagine singing without a mechanical instrument of some sort. But whether it is a piano or a live band is irrelevant to God. He authorized neither in the church's worship. Our worship must please GOD if WE are to please God. Worship is not about what man wants to offer to God; it is about what God has told man He will accept as an offering.

THE PATTERN FOR WORSHIP

Worship means a lot of things to a lot of different people. To some it is the burning of incense. To others it is a musical entertainment extravaganza. Some think that worship is purely meditation. Others prefer to think of worship as being in tune with God's creation. Worship means a lot of things to a lot of different people, but that does not make them right. All of these things, and many others, focus on men's feelings and preferences. True worship focuses on God and on what God wants.

Remember: Jesus said, "God is Spirit, and those who worship Him must worship in spirit and truth" (Jn. 4:23-24). When Jesus said that worshipping God in truth was a necessity (and the responsibility of the worshipper), then it implied the possibility of worshipping falsely, whether due to ignorance or obstinacy. There is a correct way to worship—in accordance with truth—and an incorrect way to worship—not according to truth. "Truth" refers to the fullness of what God has revealed (Jn. 1:17; 17:17). Therefore, God has revealed in His Word how He expects to be worshipped. What He has revealed is the pattern for worship He will accept. Anything offered as worship which goes beyond what God has revealed (or does not do fully what God revealed to do) will not be accepted because it cannot be in accordance with truth. Truth has limits, which means that what constitutes true worship also has limits—limits that we must respect.

No individual talent, traditional expectations, or personal preferences change God's pattern for worship. When we worship, "me, myself, and I" are not the most important considerations. When we worship, we should seek divine expectations. When we worship, we must be guided by biblical preferences. What God does not ask to be offered to Him should not be offered. What God asks to be offered should be offered in the way He asks. That is the pattern for worship and for the assembly.

THE PATTERN FOR THE LORD'S SUPPER

As Paul traveled on his journeys, he would often stop for a week in order to take the opportunity to worship with the entire local congregation. His reason for waiting, sometimes for a full week, is captured well by Luke when he wrote, "Now on the first day of the week, when the disciples came together to break bread, Paul, ready to depart the next day, spoke to them and continued his message until midnight" (Acts 20:7). Paul stayed because He wanted to partake of the Lord's Supper with these Christians. However, he had to wait until the first day of the week to do so. The early church partook of the Lord's Supper on the first day of every week as part of their worship assembly. Paul's presence did not provide a justification for holding a Thursday night communion. The pattern of the early church was to partake on Sunday, only on Sunday, and every Sunday.

When Paul rebuked the Corinthians for turning the Lord's Supper into something similar to the pagan feasts to which they were accustomed, he laid out much of the pattern for the correct manner in which the Lord's Supper should be observed. This pattern was based on the Lord's authority (1 Cor. 11:23). It includes two specified emblems, unleavened bread and grape juice (1 Cor. 11:24-25). (Remember, Christ instituted this during Passover, and this means that leavening and fermenting agents were not allowed.) It is not a meal to fill the stomach but a memorial, directing the mind toward Jesus and what He had done (1 Cor. 11:24-25). It is a declaration of faith in the atoning nature of the Messiah's death and faith that He lives still and will come again (1 Cor. 11:26). Furthermore, the failure to treat the Lord's Supper with this significance and with the accompanying reverence are sinning against the memory of Jesus (1 Cor. 11:27-29).

Some do not take the Lord's Supper every week, failing to appreciate its strength of purpose and significance. Others demean it by offering it anytime or partaking of it irreverently. The Lord's Supper is worship; therefore, we must partake of the Lord's Supper in spirit and in truth (Jn. 4:24).

THE PATTERN FOR PRAYER

Prayer is personal and corporate, private and public. Paul told the Thessalonians to "pray without ceasing" (1 Th. 5:17), while also regulating prayer in the worship assembly of the Corinthians (1 Cor. 14:15). There are those who treat prayer as an informal, casual "talk" with God while others insist that one must use "Thee" and "Thou" in order to be scriptural. The disciples recognized their need for prayer but also realized that there was a right way and a wrong way to pray. Therefore, Jesus helped immensely when He said, "In this manner therefore, pray" (Mt. 6:9a), presenting the pattern for prayer that has divine approval.

Prayer should be directed to God the Father with appropriate reverence: "Our Father which art in heaven, Hallowed be Your name" (Mt. 6:9b). We should pray for the church, which is God's kingdom now in existence: "Your kingdom come" (Mt. 6:10a). We should always pray in a manner consistent with God's will and accept God's will (1 Jn. 5:14): "Your will be done on earth as it is in heaven" (Mt. 6:10b). We should pray for needs—not wants: "Give us this day our daily bread" (Mt. 6:11). We should ask for forgiveness: "And forgive us our debts, As we forgive our debtors" (Mt. 6:12). We should ask for strength to overcome temptation: "And do not lead us into temptation, But deliver us from the evil one" (Mt. 6:13a). We should praise God: "For Yours is the kingdom and the power and the glory for ever. Amen" (Matthew 6:13b). Paul later elaborated, "Therefore I exhort first of all that supplications, prayers, intercessions, and giving of thanks be made for all men" (1 Tim. 2:1), and reminded the Ephesians that approaching God in prayer was possible only by the authority of Jesus Christ (Eph. 5:20) as our mediator (1 Tim. 2:5).

But prayer is more than a list of things. It is worship directed heavenward in accordance with God's will considered inwardly through thoughts and words expressed outwardly. It should never become ritualistic or routine, either in action or content. It is where we reach out in spirit to God who is spirit to speak to our Creator about matters of truth in accordance with the truth.

THE PATTERN FOR MUSIC

For some reason, people unfamiliar with the church are shocked when they discover that we do not use any mechanical instruments of music in our worship. This indicates, first of all, that most of their information about religious practices comes from experience and popular culture rather than the Bible. Second, this shows just how difficult it can be for people to limit themselves to the New Testament pattern.

The Bible refers to music of various sorts throughout its pages. The Old Testament refers to musical instruments serving in both secular and religious functions. The New Testament refers to Jesus and the disciples singing in worship, the church singing in worship, trumpets used in a military context, and of course a description of worship in heaven in the symbolic language of Revelation. It is important to note that only one of these categories is pertinent to the pattern of music for us today: what music the church used in worship. No other reference gives Christians authority in the music of worship. Actual scriptures referring to music in the worship of the church (both in the assembly and out) are few (Acts 16:25; 1 Cor. 14:15; Eph. 5:19; Col. 3:16; Jas. 5:13). However, the pattern provided in each instance is limited to singing.

God never approves of any musical offering from Christians other than singing a capella, a musical term that means singing without mechanical instruments of music and which, incidentally, literally means "singing in the manner of the church." Most people realize this. What they do not realize is that when they add an instrument into the music of worship, they abandon God's pattern.

THE PATTERN FOR GIVING

A lesson on giving generally draws the ire of most people, who cite it as the favorite topic of many preachers and a not so subtle attempt to suggest a raise. Of course, the way most people approach giving, who could blame them? During the eighties, televangelists called on their viewers to give sacrificially "for the Lord" while these so-called preachers used the money to build multi-million dollar homes for themselves. Many denominations teach tithing, a practice found only in the Old Testament and never in the New Testament church, in order to ensure a healthy budget. Some churches act far more seriously in regard to extracting a particular percentage from their people than they do with how the people actually live. Then there are the preachers who get up and talk about the impending budget crisis and cite a few dollar figures from the best contributors in order to try to make the rest of the people in the congregation give more out of guilt.

In the New Testament, all giving was a free-will offering. The collection was taken on the first day of the week when the saints had assembled (1 Cor. 16:1), and each person was to determine for himself what he could give, setting aside that amount specifically for the Lord's purposes (1 Cor. 16:2). What mattered to the Lord was not the dollar figure itself but the heart of the giver (Mk. 12:41-44). Of course, there are those who miss the point and take glee in pinching pennies for the Lord instead of responding with liberality in view of the Lord's own generosity (2 Cor. 9:1-2).

Giving is one form of modern-day sacrifice (Heb. 13:15-16). But the sacrifice is measured not by the amount or percentage but by whether a person has personally given "his all" (2 Cor. 8:5). "So let each one give as he purposes in his heart, not grudgingly or of necessity; for God loves a cheerful giver" (2 Cor. 9:7).

THE PATTERN FOR PREACHING

In his inspired record of the early church's work in spreading the gospel, Luke said, "Now on the first day of the week, when the disciples came together to break bread, Paul, ready to depart the next day, spoke to them and continued his message until midnight" (Acts 20:7). In the first century, when Christians gathered together, preaching was part of that assembly. While preaching was authorized and occurred at other times as well, the association with the Lord's Supper demonstrates the high place the preaching of God's Word held in the early church.

Unfortunately, the proclamation of God's Word does not receive this same respect today. Messages centered on social responsibility have replaced biblical calls for repentance, obedience, and moral responsibility. In many places you are more likely to hear a man, book, or Reader's Digest quoted as you are to hear book, chapter, and verse (Mt. 15:9). Exposition of scripture has given way to bush league psychology.

Paul told Timothy, "Preach the word! Be ready in season and out of season. Convince, rebuke, exhort, with all longsuffering and teaching" (2 Tim. 4:2). The content of preaching must be God's Word, the purpose of preaching is to correct wrong and encourage right, the required attitude is one that patiently instructs people in the ways of God, and the time to do this is all the time, in every age, to all peoples, regardless of the circumstances. There are plenty who are content to place salve on seared consciences and to scratch and tickle the ears of the obstinate. They have their reward. But a true gospel preacher follows God's pattern for preaching.

THE MEANING OF WORSHIP AND THE ASSEMBLY

What happens in the church's assembly is a hot topic in some respects today. After all, in some places you can choose between contemporary worship and traditional worship. Some churches will have a choir, while others advertise a "live band" (which, I have observed, also appears on the marquee of some bars). People are enticed by the various forms of "spontaneous" worship and, in some quarters, meditative worship. You can find just about any variation of worship that might appeal to you. We have fallen into a pep rally mentality instead of assembling to focus on God and His Word. But that is precisely the problem.

The assembly is not supposed to be focused on the preferences of the people but on the supremacy of God. Much of what goes on in the assembly today is more about entertainment than it is about Jehovah. And the people love to have it so. Rather than reflecting on the necessity and purpose of the cross during the Lord's Supper, people look for a way to still partake of the emblems while changing their meaning. We should rejoice in (or "celebrate" for you contemporary folks) the life and resurrection of Christ throughout our lives, but these are meaningless for us without pondering the cost. Lessons from the pulpit have become increasingly watered down sermonettes about as spiritually satisfying as cotton candy. It tastes sweet, but there's really not that much to it. Congregational singing has become congregational listening. Prayer in some places is a showboating extravaganza. Fundraisers are now replacing free-will offerings.

For many the assembly has become a combination concert, motivational seminar, and outlet for frustrated talent—and cheap too! This may be what people do today, but that does not make it pleasing to God. The Israelites "worshipped" Jehovah with the totems at the high places and mixed in some idolatrous imagery and practices yet still believed their worship pleased God. The same thing is true today. A reverent assembly is being replaced with pandering, and you can even buy the book to learn how to pander better. Worship is about God (Rev. 4:11), and the assembly should focus on God. When God and His will cease to be at the center of the assembly, then our reverence is vain, and we are only fooling ourselves (Mt. 15:9).

DISCUSSION QUESTIONS:

Please give at least one applicable scripture reference when answering each question.

1. What things does the Lord's church have permission to do when assembled together?

2. What is an accurate definition of worship? What biblical principles did you use to arrive at this definition?

3. Does everything we do when assembled together qualify as worship? How do you know?

4. What are the keys to worshiping God in a way that pleases Him?

5. Why do members of the New Testament church take the Lord's Supper every Sunday?

6. When we worship in song, what should the content of those songs be? Why does the Lord's church not use mechanical instruments of music when worshiping? Does this apply only when the entire congregation is assembled?

7. Should the entire congregation be involved in singing praise to God, or is it OK to just "sit back and listen" (i.e. to a choir)?

8. In a mixed assembly (men and women), why don't women take a leading role in worship (i.e. leading singing, leading prayer, serving the Lord's Supper, etc.)?

9. What should the content of our prayers be? Why do we pray to the Father and not Jesus or the Holy Spirit?

10. How much should you be giving on the first day of the week? What is your scriptural basis for determining this?

ASSIGNMENT:

Read Hebrews 10:24-25, Matthew 5:23-24, and John 4:20-24. Think about the importance of preparing to worship God (privately, or with your brethren). What are some proper ways to prepare yourself to worship? Are you doing these things now? What things do you need to change to make your worship more acceptable to God in the future?

Begin this week setting aside at least fifteen minutes to prepare yourself before coming to Bible class and the worship assembly.

What do you notice about your own attitude when you arrive and when you leave when you prepare yourself beforehand?

CHAPTER SIX:
LET'S GET BUSY

Everyone today is busy. We are busy with work. We are busy at home. Our kids are busy at school and busy with extracurricular activities, which means that parents are busier still. You will even find people who will argue over who is busier. Unfortunately, rarely are we busy in the Lord's work.

I am not sure when people decided that showing up for Bible Class and worship constituted the entirety of Christian activity. I do not know when it began, but it sure seems to have taken root. It is so much part of our thinking that we now judge people's faithfulness almost totally based upon their attendance. However, worship is not the only activity commanded by the Lord for His people. We are to be active in teaching the lost, active in strengthening the saved, and active in doing good, especially for those in need. Some of this, it is true, can be accomplished through regular meeting times. Bible classes are designed to strengthen the saved. We can bring a friend with us to worship. We can contribute toward a good cause. But the underlying attitude today often is one of fulfilling an obligation on Sunday without any effort expended the other six days of the week.

Individual souls need individual attention, whether it is a Bible study, a short visit, or a helping hand. Christianity should permeate our lives, which means that participation in the Lord's work should extend throughout the week. When there is work to do in the kingdom, we should find a way to work it in to our schedules. "If anyone desires to come after Me, let him deny himself, and take up his cross daily, and follow Me" (Lk. 9:23). We are all busy. The difference lies in what we each are busy doing.

THERE IS MUCH TO DO

Most people who have worked with others at any level have experienced the frustration of the "loafing employee." There are some people out there who seem to believe that their job is to collect a paycheck. In retail business there might be all sorts of customers milling about but this person still cannot find anything that he needs to do.

While I would not charge Christians with this level of lethargy, it remains true that many do not actively participate in the work of the church—often because they do not see anything they think they can do. This attitude demonstrates two different problems. In some cases people may be completely unprepared to do the work required, but this is due to their failure to prepare themselves—not due to the extreme difficulty of the tasks. Teaching Bible class is not easy, but how many people attend classes and seminars in order to gain or improve their skills? Many routine chores take valuable time from people who are willing to handle the more difficult assignments, yet some people are unwilling even to do these things. Others may possess the required skills but turn a blind eye to the need. They may not see it because they spend their time looking elsewhere. We need to restore a true compassion for those in need, whether that need is physical or spiritual. Every lost soul cries out, "There is much left to do!" Every wounded heart says, "Help me!" Every call for participation in the work should say to us, "I need you to be involved!"

Perhaps we need to improve in our advertising of how desperately the church needs workers. As Jesus said, "The harvest truly is plentiful, but the laborers are few. Therefore pray the Lord of the harvest to send out laborers into His harvest" (Mt. 9:37-38).

SPIRITUAL ACTIVITY WITH A SPIRITUAL EMPHASIS

If a person had never even heard the word "church" prior to entering some of the various buildings scattered throughout the land, he might have difficulty recognizing it as a spiritual entity. Congregations pepper their marquees, bulletins, and web pages with congratulatory notes, announcements about how to join the softball league, blood drives, visiting musical groups, and citizenship awards. They might include vague messages about morality, but rarely does one find distinctive doctrine and doctrine related explanations with references to the Bible. These are apparently too controversial.

The various groups that gather within a congregation often end up with a social emphasis or a performance emphasis but rarely with a spiritual or service emphasis. Why is that? Our activity defines us—not self-righteous claims. If we wish for others to see us as a people concerned with the spiritual, our activity should tell them more easily than our talk (Jas. 1:22). People are often drawn to the "busy" congregation, yet it matters immensely what keeps a congregation busy. More than once a person has explained his "church choice" according to all the things that the youth do together without considering whether or not what the youth were doing together was scriptural or spiritually beneficial.

This is not to say that the church should never socialize—far from it. However, what brings a people together and makes them one must be their mutual response to the gospel call (2 Th. 2:14) and ongoing commitment to personal spiritual maturity (2 Pet. 3:18). Without a core of spiritual activity with a spiritual emphasis, a church becomes little more than a meaningless social club with tax-deductible dues.

PEOPLE-CENTERED LIVES

Any mention of the work of the church immediately leads to the three-pronged outline of (1) evangelism (Mt. 28:18-20; Mk. 16:15), (2) edification (Eph. 4:16; 1 Cor. 14:26), and (3) benevolence (Gal. 6:10; Jas. 1:27). While these three certainly give an accurate, scriptural summation of the church's God-given activity, the approach itself lacks heart and meaning.

It is not enough to describe the church's work in such a way because so many fall into the trap of viewing the Lord's work through the prism of the treasury rather than through the glass of congregational activity. Money given most assuredly is an important factor that contributes to teaching the lost by providing funds for people to go preach the gospel, for tracts, and for needed materials. Contributions make it possible to provide support for those who spend their time studying and helping others improve their understanding of the scriptures or in purchasing materials for Bible classes. Funds from the treasury ensure that the church is able to assist those in true need. However, God did not design the church to work solely though a bank account. The church is about people: people of a particular character who live in a particular manner and interact with others in a particular way.

All three activities described here are centered on people's needs. Evangelism addresses the need for salvation. Edification addresses the need for spiritual growth. Benevolence addresses the need for both provision and caring companionship. But until we center these activities on people as individuals who have needs, our work will remain cold and distant instead of being a living testimony to the extent of God's love and the power of His Word living in us (Gal. 2:20).

GETTING INVOLVED

Associating with a congregation of God's people does not require extensive effort, though some seem to have difficulty doing so. If you are a Christian, all you must do is approach the elders or respond to the invitation to make your desire known. If you are not yet a Christian, when you obey the gospel you generally let people know simultaneously your desire to be part of that particular congregation. However, people do not always appreciate the full meaning of that association. They want to be considered part of the congregation, but they do not always want to be involved.

The purpose of a congregation of God's people is to act in concert to fulfill God's will. However, in order to act people must know what to do. Far too often people wait to be approached or do their best to avoid contact with anyone that might seek to include them more in congregational activities. But while congregations should always work to incorporate their entire membership into the plan of work, it is equally true that every member should step forward and demonstrate not only a willingness but also an eagerness to participate in that work.

What might surprise you is that getting involved in the work with your fellow Christians can be one of the most enjoyable experiences of your life. You become part of something bigger than yourself, enjoy the company of people who share your values, and improve your own focus on spiritual things. "Therefore, my beloved brethren, be steadfast, immovable, always abounding in the work of the Lord, knowing that your labor is not in vain in the Lord" (1 Cor. 15:58).

YOU DON'T NEED A PROGRAM

I am not against programs. Not at all. A congregation can benefit immensely by a good evangelism program or visitation program. If you are to have any order to your congregational Bible study, you will gain by having an actual Bible Class program. Programs are very helpful—if we understand what they are, what they do, and what they cannot do.

A program simply expresses the ordered manner in which Christians go about doing a particular work. An evangelism program itself cannot teach a single soul; it provides a structure by which those who are willing to teach the gospel in some manner are more easily informed of those who wish to learn and sometimes the training needed for those who require it (Mk. 16:15). Likewise, a visitation program does not visit anyone; it provides the means by which people who will visit learn who might need a visit (Mt. 25:31-46). No matter what the program might be, it is meaningless without people who demonstrate a willingness to do the work. A congregation could have a program for everything under the sun, but that alone does not mean that anyone is actually working. A program's value is measured in manpower—not in its title or stated goals.

Most of all, Christians must realize that they do not need a program in place in order to work. You can evangelize and visit without a program. The program helps individuals understand how their work is a part of the whole, but a congregation can please God without any official program in place. In fact, if Christians dedicated themselves and motivated themselves to all of these various activities, a program would become superfluous. You don't need to be involved in a program to please God, but you do have to be involved in the work (1 Cor. 15:58).

YOU ARE NOT ALONE

Many young Christians are so filled with enthusiasm for the Lord following their conversion that they attack the work with vigor and await any opportunity to volunteer. They sometimes complain about the complacency they perceive among the rest of the congregation. They want to get involved but then sometimes conclude that they are the only ones that are interested in working. They struggle for a while, then finally either become so disheartened that they abandon the Lord or find their place among the rest of the people who tried once to do something but finally gave up.

It is important that the Lord sent His disciples out in pairs (Lk. 10:1). Fellowship in the work is the strongest way to overcome judging everything by the numbers. When we go visiting with our brethren, whatever the outcome of the visit, we can gain strength and feel good about doing the work of the Lord. When we preach the gospel to the lost, it helps to have a brother or sister there to encourage us and keep us from doubting our ability or blaming ourselves for the lack of positive response (1 Cor. 3:6).

There are few things that would ever get done in the Lord's church if it all depended upon just one person. Yet many things do not get done because many people do not get involved—primarily because they are convinced they would have to do it all by themselves. But we must be willing to offer our services and our company to others who are working. We must be willing to ask others to join us in doing the work. Many people feel lonely in the work because they never invite anyone to join them. But in the Lord's church, you are never alone.

DISCUSSION QUESTIONS:

1. What kinds of activities do Christians need to be involved in?

2. God blesses everyone with different abilities. What are some talents you possess that could be used scripturally to benefit the work of the Lord in your "home" congregation?

3. Are you aware of the various "programs" in the congregation where you work and worship? (In other words, what is your congregation busy doing?)

4. How did you learn about these activities? How might they be better advertised so that others who are interested could find out about them?

5. What else could the leaders of this congregation do to encourage involvement?

6. Why is it so important to get "plugged in" to the work of a local congregation?

7. Since you obeyed the gospel, have you ever felt like you were alone in your struggles to live as a Christian?

8. What can you do to help those you know who are still in need of salvation?

9. What can you do to help those who need to grow spiritually?

10. What can you do to find out more about the needs people have?

ASSIGNMENT:

Find one of the faithful members of the congregation where you attend whom you know to be involved in several different aspects of the Lord's work. Ask them for suggestions about what you could do to become more involved. Come back to our study with a report on what you learned and what you want to get more involved in. Then, take some of that sound advice and get involved!

CHAPTER SEVEN:
WHO ARE THESE PEOPLE?

Becoming part of the church has two very different aspects. First, one's obedience to the gospel not only saves but also adds you to the church (Acts 2:38; 1 Cor. 12:13). "And the Lord added to the church daily those who were being saved" (Acts 2:47b). So a new Christian is part of the church in conjunction with salvation. However, to be considered part of the church and to feel that you belong are two separate things. After all, you may know only a few people in the local congregation. Understanding what you share in common is the quickest way to create a meaningful bond among people, and this is certainly true for the church.

Christians share the most important things in life: love for God, obedience to the gospel, respect for God's authority, the hope of heaven, and the same value system. Therefore, while people are at different levels of maturity and commitment, you immediately share a worldview that has Christ at the center and includes a certain type of predictable behavior (1 Tim. 3:15). While you will discover weaknesses in individuals as time goes by, you can become comfortable with the core of what makes these people God's people (1 Pet. 2:9-10).

The church is made up of Christians—those who have chosen and demonstrated submission to Christ (Eph. 5:23-25). They are much like you: learning, struggling, and growing. They are individuals who have chosen to become part of something far more important than themselves. While it is important to get to know people on an individual basis, it is always important to remember that it is not our individuality that brings us together but Christ and His Word (Jn. 6:44-45; 8:32; 17:17; Eph. 4:16).

MEET YOUR NEW FAMILY

For the new Christian, getting to know his new brothers and sisters can prove to be a challenge all its own. You can know the faces, and you can know the names, but these people are not just entries in a directory but the individuals on whom a babe in Christ must learn to rely and with whom he will discover his closest friendships and associations.

The apostle Paul wrote, "Be kindly affectionate to one another with brotherly love, in honor giving preference to one another" (Rom. 12:10). Both terms Paul used imply a family relationship—a devotion to one another built upon a common bond, a common purpose, and a common character. Jesus said, "A new commandment I give to you, that you love one another; as I have loved you, that you also love one another. By this all will know that you are My disciples, if you have love for one another" (Jn. 13:34-35). A dedication to cause and comrades previously reserved for men bound together by a common experience in war now exists among a people dedicated to their Savior. But part of being family is the willingness to help one another through tough times, and a spiritual family helps one another through spiritual problems. "Confess your trespasses to one another, and pray for one another, that you may be healed. The effective, fervent prayer of a righteous man avails much" (Jas. 5:16). It takes far less care to loan a child some money than it does to help him have the humility and strength to admit his weaknesses.

While it takes time and effort to get to know everyone in a congregation, the better you know them, and the better they know you, the better you can help one another.

EVERYBODY HAS A ROLE

In his first epistle to the Corinthians, the apostle Paul wrote, "For in fact the body is not one member but many. If the foot should say, "Because I am not a hand, I am not of the body," is it therefore not of the body? And if the ear should say, "Because I am not an eye, I am not of the body," is it therefore not of the body? If the whole body were an eye, where would be the hearing? If the whole were hearing, where would be the smelling? But now God has set the members, each one of them, in the body just as He pleased. And if they were all one member, where would the body be? But now indeed there are many members, yet one body. " (1 Cor. 12:14-20). Although Paul's discussion centered on the importance of all types of miraculous gifts, his illustration demonstrates an important principle: everybody has a role.

Unfortunately, some people have trouble understanding value or importance in any way other than holding a prominent position (3 Jn. 9-10). Such people are interested in power, control, and accolades rather than the service that defines every role one might have within the church, beginning even with Jesus Himself. "For even the Son of Man did not come to be served, but to serve, and to give His life a ransom for many" (Mk. 10:45).

In Christianity we must set aside ambition and take up aspirations. Self is no longer the most important consideration; God's will, the church, and others all take priority (Mt. 6:33; Phil. 2:3-4). The church needs leaders and followers, workers and helpers. Not everyone can be in the forefront, but everybody has an important role.

ELDERS: SHEPHERDS OF SPIRITUAL CARE

If a new Christian has not previously become acquainted with the elders in the congregation where he attends, this should be one of his first priorities. Likewise, elders should make it one of their first priorities to get to know new members of the congregation (1 Th. 5:12-13). The purpose for this is not to reinforce some power structure or to "network" but rather to begin a healthy relationship whereby the elders can learn the strengths and weaknesses, talents and needs of the new Christian in order to help him grow spiritually and become an integral part of the congregation.

In his first epistle Peter wrote, "The elders who are among you I exhort, I who am a fellow elder and a witness of the sufferings of Christ, and also a partaker of the glory that will be revealed: Shepherd the flock of God which is among you, serving as overseers, not by compulsion but willingly, not for dishonest gain but eagerly; nor as being lords over those entrusted to you, but being examples to the flock; and when the Chief Shepherd appears, you will receive the crown of glory that does not fade away" (1 Pet. 5:1-4). Elders are therefore not a board of directors who hand down decisions in memos and whose main purpose is to keep the church in the black. Elders are spiritual shepherds whose work it is to ensure the best spiritual nourishment, protection, and environment possible for the flock, while also helping individual members overcome their personal spiritual struggles.

Elders are the men who want you to go to heaven. They will teach, correct, visit, and do whatever it takes to help you achieve that end. "Therefore take heed to yourselves and to all the flock, among which the Holy Spirit has made you overseers, to shepherd the church of God which He purchased with His own blood" (Acts 20:28). With this in mind, we should heed the words of the writer of Hebrews: "Obey those who rule over you, and be submissive, for they watch out for your souls, as those who must give account. Let them do so with joy and not with grief, for that would be unprofitable for you" (Heb. 13:17).

DEACONS: SERVANTS OF SPECIAL RESPONSIBILITY

Deacons often get lost in the shuffle in the Lord's church, which is truly sad because of how important they are to the success of a local congregation. Paul specifically referred to deacons along with bishops (elders) in Philippians 1:1, showing they have a special role and responsibility in the local congregation—a responsibility that is different from the elders but a responsibility that is greater than the average member. The men who serve well as deacons deserve great admiration, as do their families, because deacons are men given the tough assignments and the ongoing responsibilities in the church to keep everything going smoothly, while allowing the elders the time to concentrate on spiritual shepherding.

The word translated "deacon" is diakonos, a term that is also translated "minister" on many occasions. It refers to a person who has made the commitment to fulfill various duties and obligations that are determined by someone else.

Deacons are NOT junior elders, but deacons must be men that elders can trust—in their faithfulness to God, their work in the church, and their respect for the elders' role as well as their own. Deacons are people that the church can count on to get the job done—whatever that job might be. They are ready to accept responsibility—both when they are needed for a work and afterwards. This is a great responsibility and the reason why they must be qualified (1 Tim. 3:8-12).

When you realize all the different responsibilities that a deacon might receive, you might well wonder why anyone would be willing to give up so much time and effort on a voluntary basis. Paul provides the best answer: "For those who have served well as deacons obtain for themselves a good standing and great boldness in the faith which is in Christ Jesus" (1 Tim. 3:13).

TEACHERS: STUDENTS WHO SACRIFICE AND SHARE

Quality Bible class teachers are some of the unsung heroes of the church. They volunteer to take on an additional workload of study, preparation, and possibly handwork in order to help other Christians and other Christians' children grow in faith so that they might one day enjoy the beauty of heaven's reward.

Teaching God's Word is a tremendous responsibility—regardless of the age group a person has. James wrote, "My brethren, let not many of you become teachers, knowing that we shall receive a stricter judgment" (Jas. 3:1). It is an honor and privilege to teach a Bible Class, but it is also a responsibility. A teacher must study and prepare well enough to make sure that the lesson taught is completely in line with God's truth (Jn. 8:32) while also showing care for the students. A good Bible Class teacher is far more than knowledgeable. That teacher must have character that encourages attention, questions, and comments. A good teacher is committed to learning and then sharing as much as possible of all that he or she has learned, according to how much the age group can handle. This alone requires both good understanding and judgment.

In reference to the qualities necessary for teaching the Bible, James said, "But the wisdom that is from above is first pure, then peaceable, gentle, willing to yield, full of mercy and good fruits, without partiality and without hypocrisy" (Jas. 3:17). These characteristics are essential for the teacher because they insure that the student's best interests are in mind rather than the teacher's. Good Bible Class teachers are one of the most valuable assets a congregation can have. They should be treated accordingly.

WORSHIP LEADERS

While many have written about the nature of worship as directed by God in the New Testament, very few give adequate attention to those who lead in worship, yet the New Testament addresses this subject seriously and establishes a standard for worship leaders that generally exceeds what we ourselves practice. Leading in worship is a privilege—not a right. It is a responsibility—not a position of honor. Leading in worship is not about "being up front" or being "prominent," though these are indeed natural outcomes from leading in worship. Leading in worship is about service, and God has specified those who are qualified to serve Him in this capacity.

In his first epistle to the Corinthians, Paul said, "Let your women keep silent in the churches, for they are not permitted to speak; but they are to be submissive, as the law also says. And if they want to learn something, let them ask their own husbands at home; for it is shameful for women to speak in church" (1 Cor. 14:34-35). In this context the apostle had mentioned specifically the public functions of praying, singing, speaking, and translating in worship. God has spoken clearly that women may not serve in the capacity of worship leader (1 Tim. 2:9-15). But this is not the only restriction God makes. Paul also told Timothy, "I desire therefore that the men pray everywhere, lifting up holy hands, without wrath and doubting" (1 Tim. 2:8). Those who lead in worship must be men of integrity ("holy"), men of high character, and men who fully understand the significance and responsibilities attached to standing before others while leading in worship.

God wants spiritually minded men to lead prayer, students of the word to teach, song leaders who reflect on the meaning of the songs to lead singing, men who are willing to give to collect the offering, and men who fully appreciate the sacrifice of Christ to serve at His table. Worship leaders should be examples of Christianity, so that should their friends attend they would not be shocked to find them reverently and humbly serving. Leading in worship does not come by right of membership but by means of developed spiritual character.

PREACHERS-NOT PASTORS

The religious world as a whole tends to confuse the roles of preachers and pastors. The New Testament uses the terms bishop, elder, and pastor (as well as the related verbs) to refer to the position of spiritual service where a plurality of men oversee the spiritual well-being of a congregation while describing the person whose main role is to proclaim the message and teach the gospel as preacher, minister of the gospel, and evangelist. Most people do not see this distinction or do not think it is a big deal, but in following the pattern of the New Testament, maintaining the proper roles is essential for the spiritual health of God's people. Pastors have qualifications not required of preachers (1 Tim. 3:1-7; Tit. 1:5-9). While some qualities overlap, they are not the same, and the roles are not the same.

A preacher's primary responsibility is the faithful proclamation of the Word of God (2 Tim. 4:2-4). By implication, then, he must spend time diligently seeking out that truth in order to communicate it to others (1 Tim. 4:13-16). The communication of the word involves sermons, Bible classes, personal evangelism, writing, and even counseling (2 Th. 2:14-15). A preacher is a member of the local congregation and submits to the leadership of the eldership, even though he is responsible for teaching in regard to both the qualifications and work of the elders in seeing that a congregation follows God's pattern when qualified men are present in the congregation (Tit. 1:5). He makes visits to those in need as any other member should (Jas. 1:27) and should present a good example of the Christianity he is proclaiming (1 Tim. 4:12).

The preacher is indeed in the most visible role in a congregation. He is the one who stands before the congregation every week, the one most likely to keep office hours, and usually the one who is most visible in the community as a "representative" of the church. However, despite this obvious visibility, it is important for Christians to respond to their spiritual shepherds, the elders, and discuss their problems and spiritual needs with them. Preaching is about the message, pastoring about the people. Both are spiritual works with spiritual concerns and spiritual purposes, but the roles are different. A man may serve in both roles if he is qualified, but such an undertaking is a heavy workload indeed. Those who are able to do so well deserve both our admiration and our thanks (1 Tim. 5:17).

NO TITLE NECESSARY

In many places and for many years titles defined a person within a church community. Most denominational pastors prefer the title "Reverend" unless they wish to advertise their education and like "Dr." instead. In the more ecumenical crowd, "Father," "Bishop," and the like are the designations of choice, despite Christ's own condemnation of the employment of using religious titles in order to create a clergy class—something simply not found in scripture (Mt. 23:1-12). This is not to mention the way in which most people completely confuse the scriptural designations of elders (Acts 20:17-31)—presbyters and bishops—to create a church hierarchy or the changing of the servant role of deacon described in scripture (1Tim. 3:8-13) to one of church decision maker.

There are indeed people who bear designations in various congregations of the Lord's church—including elders, deacons, preachers, teachers, and even worship leaders. However, these designations are specific to roles bearing specific responsibilities in the activity of the church. They carry absolutely no titular authority but only authority necessary to perform their responsibilities in accordance with God's authority. This is important so that every Christian understands he is as important to God as anyone else (Rom. 12:3-4).

You do not need a title to be important. I am simultaneously saddened and amused by the laundry list of titles associated with some congregations. You do not have to carry the title Music Minister (or Praise leader) to lead singing. I hope we realize that it is unnecessary to give the janitor the title "Minister of Mess." Titles do not really matter. What matters is carrying out the work of the Lord, and to this we should give our all.

DISCUSSION QUESTIONS:

Please list at least one appropriate scripture reference with each of your answers.

1. Do you think that most people your age really feel like they belong as members of their home congregations? Why or why not? What can be done to help all members feel like they are really part of the "church family"?

2. Do you already "prefer" your brethren to worldly people, or is this an area where you need some work (Rom. 12:10)? What are some appropriate ways to show a real preference for your brethren?

3. What responsibilities do members of this spiritual family—the church— have for each other? In what ways have your brothers and sisters in Christ helped you?

4. Jesus commanded all His followers to "seek first the kingdom of God" (Matt. 6:33). What is the "kingdom of God" and how are you supposed to seek it?

5. What is the proper role of an elder? Who is qualified to serve as an elder?

6. What is the proper role of a deacon? Who is qualified to serve as a deacon?

7. What is the proper role of a teacher? Who is qualified to serve as a teacher?

8. What is the proper role of a worship leader? Who is qualified to serve as a worship leader?

9. What is the proper role of a preacher? Who is qualified to serve as a preacher?

10. Why doesn't the church of Christ use titles such as "Reverend" or "Father" to define the different roles that its members have?

ASSIGNMENT:

What does the phrase "everybody has a role" really mean? What role do you currently have in your local congregation of the Lord's church? What role(s) would you like to have in the future? What will you have to do to become "qualified" for those additional areas of service?

This week make sure to meet your elders, deacons, preacher(s), and Bible Class teachers. Ask each of them what they find most difficult about their role and then bring your list back for next week to discuss.

CHAPTER EIGHT:
NOBODY'S PERFECT

Nobody's perfect. Isn't that what everyone says? And it is almost true. After all, Paul told the Romans, "As it is written, There is none righteous, no, not one" (Rom. 3:10), later concluding, "for all have sinned and fall short of the glory of God" (Rom. 3:23). But some people apparently believe that by saying, "Nobody's perfect," it somehow excuses their personal imperfection and makes it acceptable. This is far from what Paul meant. It is essential for all of us to recognize that we have sinned and therefore cannot lay claim to any moral superiority. We have sinned and must pay that price regardless of how small it may seem in comparison to others' sin (Jas. 2:10).

Sadly, a people once forgiven can forget that this is the foundation of their pleasing God, rather than their own personal record, intelligence, or financial contributions. As soon as we begin to think and act as if we or anyone else is perfect, we are heading for a fall. "Pride goes before destruction, and a haughty spirit before a fall" (Prov. 16:18). We all need God's Word to guide us because we all proved inadequate in plotting our own course through life (Jer. 10:23). It is a shame that some people need to be reminded of their spiritual failures to keep returning them to a humble submission to God's Word. "Therefore let him who thinks he stands take heed lest he fall" (1 Cor. 10:12).

Nobody is perfect except for Christ. Therefore, all of our efforts should be directed by His Will and for His glory. Our trust must no longer be in ourselves, in the world's ideas, or in the men around us but rather solely and completely in Him who died for us.

GREAT EXPECTATIONS

It is good and proper to have high expectations when you become a Christian. You should expect the greatest blessings ever offered to mankind. You should expect to learn much about what God expects from you. You should expect to be challenged to reach great personal heights in your spiritual life. And you should expect to find people who love you like family within the church. These are great expectations, but they are also reasonable.

But sometimes our expectations can get us into trouble if they do not reflect God's will and certain realities. Simon the former sorcerer observed that the ability to do miracles was made possible by the laying on of hands by an apostle and immediately expected both that he had a right to that power and that it could be bought (Acts 8:17-18). His expectations were skewed by his previous belief system, creating great expectations that were completely unreasonable and contrary to God's will. Some young Christians believe that everything will be perfect in the church, that everyone is always on his best behavior and that there are no problems, disagreements, or occasional sins. These expectations are harmful because they create a false standard by which to measure other people. We can have great expectations about the church while still recognizing that all people have to repent of sin from time to time, even after they become Christians (1 Jn. 1:8-10).

Great expectations can hurt you if they do not match what God has revealed. Sometimes we allow ignorance to create expectations so unreasonable that they become obstacles to our faith. Therefore, we must also make sure to learn what God's expectations are, fully and completely, and then personally rise to meet them.

TEMPTATION PERSISTS, SO YOU MUST RESIST

I am not sure why, but many people seem to believe that after they become Christians the devil will leave them alone. Nothing could be further from the truth. While your obedience to the gospel provides forgiveness of your past sins and makes you a Christian (Heb. 5:8-9; Acts 22:16), this is only the beginning of the battle. Satan is not going to throw in the towel just because you were baptized. That was just round one.

James addressed the problems temptation can cause in our lives, but he also pointed out that we can grow from the experience by gaining confidence in how to address those temptations and thereby mature spiritually (Jas. 1:2-4). Sometimes we can think we have stronger faith than we actually do simply because a particular temptation has yet to present itself. But if Satan thinks it might drive a wedge in our faith, he will try it (Jas. 1:9-11).

Satan will do anything he can to entice us to fall from the grace we have been allowed to enjoy (Gal. 5:4; Eph. 2:8-9). But knowing the blessings of salvation and the joys of Christianity, we should press ever forward in our quest to please the Savior who overcame all temptation (Heb. 4:15) and died to make these things possible.

The best way to confront temptation is to busy ourselves with learning and doing God's will. The more consumed we are with our Christianity the fewer opportunities we give Satan to attack our faith. As James wrote again, "Therefore, submit to God. Resist the devil and he will flee from you. Draw near to God and He will draw near to you" (Jas. 4:7-8a).

YES, THERE ARE HYPOCRITES

One of the saddest moments in a young Christian's life is the realization that some Christians are hypocrites. For those who have grown far too accustomed to this reality it may appear to be no big deal, but to someone young in the faith who has found the precious jewel of truth there are few things as discouraging as being a witness to a fellow Christian's hypocrisy.

Jesus described the spiritual reality of hypocrisy better than anyone else: "Woe to you, scribes and Pharisees, hypocrites! For you are like whitewashed tombs which indeed appear beautiful outwardly, but inside are full of dead men's bones and all uncleanness" (Mt. 23:27). Sadly, as there were among the scribes and Pharisees, some Christians are hypocrites, just playing the role of a Christian from time to time instead of developing the character and life of a Christian for all times. However, many people empower these hypocrites by allowing the sins of these people to affect their own obedience, their own faithfulness, and their own salvation. When this happens, the young Christian who was originally so offended by the other person's hypocrisy has himself become a hypocrite.

We must commit ourselves to Jesus Christ and His Word so that even if those closest to us turned out to be hypocrites it would not affect our faith. Do not judge the value of the New Testament and of Christianity by the poorest of examples. Instead place your trust in God's revealed Word and what it says regardless of the actions of the people around you (Mt. 23:1-3). Hypocrisy is a problem; that is the truth. But a hypocrite is no more lost than the person who just gives up.

NOT PERFECT-FORGIVEN AND GROWING

When the beloved apostle Paul, a man who worked tirelessly in the kingdom and who proved to be a wonderful example of mature Christianity, wrote his first epistle to Timothy, he told this young preacher, "This is a faithful saying and worthy of all acceptance, that Christ Jesus came into the world to save sinners, of whom I am chief" (1 Tim. 1:15). Despite all his years of labor, despite all his spiritual knowledge, despite all the persecution he endured, Paul still considered himself the chiefest of sinners. This was not a comment on the man he had become but about the man he still remembered he had been, knowing that those sins would have been held against him had it not been for the sacrifice of Jesus Christ and his obedience to the gospel (Eph. 1:7; Acts 2:38).

Paul was not caught up in depression over his past; he simply retained that knowledge to have the correct perspective about his life. He was not, and would never be, perfect. He had sinned, as we all have (Rom. 3:23), and was therefore worthy of death (Rom. 6:23). But he also had been forgiven (Acts 22:16), and that made all the difference. Christians should never forget the need they had for forgiveness and what it cost Jesus for them to receive it. But we should also reflect on the beauty of being forgiven as we struggle to mature our faith (1 Pet. 2:1-3). Christians are not perfect people; they are forgiven people. They still make mistakes; they still sin from time to time (1 Jn. 1:8-10). But they have changed their course and have committed to the path of righteousness.

A new Christian must realize that his brethren are not perfect anymore than he is. But he should also know that they are the ones who are seeking that higher ground of faithfulness, dedication, and character (Phil. 3:13-14; 2 Pet. 3:18), and this quality is what makes it possible for Christians, new and old, to have such beautiful fellowship. Not all Christians are at the same place in their spiritual lives (1 Cor. 3:1-3; Heb. 5:12), but they all began the same way (Jn. 3:3-5; Mt. 28:18-20), and they are all committed to going the same direction with the rest of their lives (Rev. 2:10; 2 Tim. 4:6-8).

DISCUSSION QUESTIONS:

1. We have already discussed the problems with the phrase, "Nobody's perfect." The expression "practice makes perfect" is almost as common in our society. Does this agree or disagree with what is taught in Scripture?

2. What "great expectations" do you have for yourself spiritually?

3. How "strong" do you expect yourself to be as a Christian one year from now? Five years from now? Twenty-five years from now? What are you going to need to do along the way to achieve those goals?

4. In general, under what circumstances are you (or will you be) most vulnerable to temptations?

5. Overcoming temptation involves changing patterns of behavior. How do you escape destructive behavior patterns and create positive ones?

6. What spiritual problems in your life are most likely to recur?

7. Why does hypocrisy seem to be so common? Is there a problem with our definition of hypocrisy?

8. Do you believe that hypocrisy is more of a problem than other sins, or is it usually just a convenient excuse to lower our own standards?

9. Do you find it difficult to be patient with yourself when it comes to spiritual growth? What are the main differences between growth and maturity?

10. How do you continue to develop faith in God's forgiveness after you become a Christian? How can Christians guard against taking that forgiveness for granted?

ASSIGNMENT:

This week, take some real time to think about how important it was for Christ Jesus to live a perfect life and how He must have struggled to achieve it (Hebrews 4:15; 1 Peter 2:21-22). What effect should this have upon us as Christians?

Ask a more mature Christian in the congregation you are closer to what temptation he or she struggles with and how this has changed over the years.

CHAPTER NINE:
YOU'RE DIFFERENT, BUT IN A GOOD WAY

In the King James Version of the Bible, the apostle Peter referred to his Christian readers as "a peculiar people." Some have taken this to mean that Christians are inherently weird, strange, and odd. And though that may indeed be how the world views Christians, it is not what Peter had in mind. The text in which this reference appears sheds light on the beautiful and rich meaning of this quite misunderstood phrase. "But you are a chosen generation, a royal priesthood, a holy nation, His own special people, that you may proclaim the praises of Him who called you out of darkness into His marvelous light; who once were not a people but are now the people of God, who had not obtained mercy but now have obtained mercy" (1 Pet. 2:9-10).

Peter chose four designations by which to describe the church, but his full intent is often lost. Here, Peter is making an allusion to the history of Israel and the acceptance of a covenant with God: "Now therefore, if you will indeed obey My voice and keep My covenant, then you shall be a special treasure to Me above all people; for all the earth is Mine. And you shall be to Me a kingdom of priests and a holy nation" (Ex. 19:5-6a). So, even from the beginning, what made Israel a "peculiar people" was its relationship with God (Dt. 14:2), and this special relationship, gained through God's mercy and our obedience (Eph. 2:4; Heb. 5:8-9), is what makes the church God's people today (cf. Hos. 2:23; Acts 2:41-47)

Should we be different as Christians? Yes, indeed! Our worldview, our outlook, our behavior, and our hope should all change for the better. But the greatest difference is that we now belong to God, and that makes all the difference. "Blessed is the nation whose God is the LORD, The people He has chosen as His own inheritance" (Ps. 33:12).

THE NEW YOU

When Paul wrote to the Romans, he emphasized that the gospel is not just the means of salvation from sin but also a primer on personal transformation through the application of spiritual principles. To be saved from sin you must leave sin behind (Rom. 6:1-2), not only through the forgiveness obtained through immersion in water (Acts 2:38) but also as you emerge from the water to enter a relationship with Christ (Gal. 3:26-27) through which all Christians receive the benefit of His sacrificial death on our behalf (Rom. 6:3). Paul then concludes, "Therefore we were buried with Him through baptism into death, that just as Christ was raised from the dead by the glory of the Father, even so we also should walk in newness of life" (Rom. 6:4).

The resurrection of Christ is THE pivotal point in making Christianity a reality. The resurrection was proof of Christ's character, that He was unworthy of death. In Paul's figure he uses Jesus' resurrection to new life to illustrate the new quality of spiritual life a Christian should strive to make a day-to-day reality. This "newness of life" is not just a fresh start; it is a life of completely different character built on a very different foundation (1 Cor. 3:11).

When we obeyed the gospel, we agreed with Christ that our old life in sin was NOT right and NOT the answer. Looking to Him in faith we also agreed that His way of life, supported by the strength of His resurrection, is the only answer. People should be able to tell a difference between who you were without Christ and who you are with Christ. The new you may stumble into sin from time to time, but the new you does not allow sin to become master ever again

(Rom. 6:6). "Therefore, if anyone is in Christ, he is a new creation; old things have passed away; behold, all things have become new" (2 Cor. 5:17).

MORAL DISTINCTIVENESS

We live in a world where God's name used in vain has become the most popular form of expression, where homosexuality is called "an alternative lifestyle," and where we have categories for depictions of women in various stages of undress. Most of the world has bought into the moral relativism of postmodern pluralism (Say that three times, really fast!) so that "I'm okay, you're okay" is now considered enlightened thought and brilliant theology. However, Paul brilliantly demonstrated the intellectual poverty of the so-called wisdom of the world (1 Cor. 1:18-20), and the apostle Peter was correct when He called this ignorance (1 Pet. 1:14). Living in such a world as this, Christians have every opportunity to stand out from the crowd by standing up for righteousness. But that must begin with our own lives. Peter continued, "but as He who called you is holy, you also be holy in all your conduct, because it is written, 'Be holy, for I am holy'" (1 Pet. 1:15-16).

At the heart of holiness is a dedication to moral distinctiveness. This is the Christian's best answer to worldly thinking. Our commitment to holiness means that we refuse to accept a secular worldview, the mores of society, or the pressures to conform to or even accept immorality as normal.

No doubt the world will criticize us—not because of our moral failings but because of our moral stand (Jn. 3:18-21). But this is not a reason to fear or conform; it is an opportunity to let our light shine for Christ (Mt. 5:14-16). As the world grows darker from the blackness of sin, we should stand out even more. And that is a good thing.

COPING WITH PEER PRESSURE

Everyone must face pressure from one's peers at some point. Though often talked about as a problem solely among youth, peer pressure exists throughout life. You do not outgrow peer pressure. However, you can learn to handle it properly, which should be the goal for all who seek Christ's will in their lives (Rom. 12:1-2).

Peer pressure takes many forms, but its heart is always directed toward conformity among men in order to please men based upon the standards of men. Jesus' own work felt the cold bite of peer pressure. "Nevertheless even among the rulers many believed in Him, but because of the Pharisees they did not confess Him, lest they should be put out of the synagogue; for they loved the praise of men more than the praise of God" (Jn. 12:42-43). Social pressure from Jesus' outspoken critics caused even "leaders" to shy away from the Savior. Perhaps they feared the loss of their position socially or the loss of influence. Regardless of their own reasoning, they gave higher priority to pleasing men and fitting in among men than they did to the truth and to having fellowship with God.

It is not easy to be the only one in a crowd standing up for the truth. It is harder still when other Christians are there but are unwilling to stand with you. But the pressure exerted in these circumstances—at school, at work, or even in the church—must never sway us from our loyalty to Christ. When we stand with Jesus, we can always hold our heads high without fear. If friends leave us because of our faith, they are the ones who lost (1 Pet. 4:1-6). We should never be ashamed of Christ, lest we give Him a reason to be ashamed of us.

FINDING NEW FRIENDS

The apostle Paul told the Corinthians, "Be not be deceived: 'Evil company corrupts good habits" (1 Cor. 15:33). The problem for many young Christians, as well as those who have only recently turned back to Christ, is that evil companions are the only friends they have. These non-Christian friends have little or no real understanding of the truth and often even less patience with people who have committed their lives to it. As Peter said, "In regard to these, they think it strange that you do not run with them in the same flood of dissipation, speaking evil of you" (1 Pet. 4:4). As a result, rather than having time to enjoy their newfound freedom from sin, babes in Christ often have to confront significant peer pressure from the outset.

If having the faith to stand up for Christ when having to stand alone is difficult for any Christian, it must be overwhelming for one who just made that commitment. While one would like to have the right kind of influence upon those friends who have yet to obey the gospel, we must also prepare for the dangerous assaults that often accompany a commitment to Christ. Therefore, it is essential for new Christians to develop close friendships with other Christians quickly, learning to depend upon them for strength, support, and guidance from the scriptures from the very beginning. And mature Christians should offer their friendship and support from the beginning.

Paul told the Christians in Rome, "Be kindly affectionate to one another with brotherly love, in honor giving preference to one another" (Rom. 12:10). The more we help one another in our stand against the world, including—at times—those who used to be friends, the stronger our own bonds of friendship will become.

THE PERFECT SUPPORT GROUP

Everyone needs support. We may try to deny it from time to time, but the reality still exists and rears its head in times of turmoil when we least expect it. People in the world have recognized the value of having support to help meet various struggles in life. Specialty support groups now exist for people in almost any situation and facing various kinds of difficulties. But while these efforts have value in their place, they can never replace the greatest support ever conceived: the church of our dear Lord.

How sad it is that many Christians fail to take advantage of the strength and support offered by the local congregation, for God designed it with this in mind. "And let us consider one another in order to stir up love and good works, not forsaking the assembling of ourselves together, as is the manner of some, but exhorting one another, and so much the more as you see the Day approaching" (Heb. 10:24-25). Every time a congregation assembles Christians have the opportunity to lean on one another for support as they collectively place their confidence in God.

The church is the perfect support group because it consists of people who admit their imperfections and needs while also having strengths to offer one another. The church has members who have problems like yours but also members who have addressed those temptations successfully from whom you can learn. Most of all, the church is filled with people who care. "Rejoice with those who rejoice, and weep with those who weep" (Rom. 12:15). No one person in the church has all the answers, but we all have learned Whom to ask to get them.

DISCUSSION QUESTIONS:

1. Do you ever feel "peculiar" as a new Christian?

2. Overall—now that you have been a Christian for a short time—what has been the reaction of your friends and family to your "new life"? What differences have they noticed in you?

3. Why is the resurrection of Christ "THE pivotal point in making Christianity a reality" in a Christian's life?

4. We should recognize that there is no such thing as a "perfect Christian." With that in mind, is there a magic number of times you can sin as a Christian and have it be OK? What is the difference between stumbling and sinning from time to time and allowing sin to become your master again?

5. How would you define "holiness"? How is it possible for an imperfect person to be holy?

6. Why is "peer pressure" such a problem? Do you believe that peer pressure is more difficult to handle at certain ages than others? Is peer pressure ever a positive thing?

7. Would cutting off all ties with "those you knew before" ever be the correct way to cope with the temptations you have as a new Christian? What is the correct way to handle "old friends" who are pressuring you to go back to the life of sin you just escaped?

8. Why is it so important to share close friendships and fellowship with other Christians?

9. Why do you think that some Christians do not take advantage of the support system offered by the church?

10. In what ways could the congregation here better support you as a Christian?

ASSIGNMENT:

Make a list of all the people you have met in your home congregation so far. Begin with those whose names you can remember. (A pictorial directory would help this immensely. Check to see if your home congregation provides one.) In the coming weeks, try to learn at least the names of 2-5 "new" people each week. Remember that this is a long-term project. Be patient. Try to enjoy getting to know your new family members so that we can better support each other along the way to heaven!

CHAPTER TEN: CHRISTIANITY IS MORE THAN THEORY

Many people seem to convert to a religious theory rather than to a worldview and belief system that affects every aspect of their lives. They want the comforts of salvation without its accompanying responsibilities. This is completely unacceptable to God. Christianity is more than theory, or at least it had better be!

In his first epistle to Timothy, Paul told the young evangelist, "Let no one despise your youth, but be an example to the believers in word, in conduct, in love, in spirit, in faith, in purity" (1 Tim. 4:12). If Christianity were only about information or a theory about life, Timothy's behavior would have been irrelevant. It is precisely because the gospel delivers instruction in behavior, with the expectation that people adopt that behavior, which made Timothy's personal behavior so important. He had to give more than just a recitation of the message; he needed to model the message for his hearers.

We must commit ourselves to Christian living—not just New Testament theory. Jesus did not live a theoretical life, die a theoretical death, or achieve a theoretical victory. It is the historical reality of these events that give power to the message founded upon them, and it is by our actions that we demonstrate solidarity with and commitment to the One who died (Heb. 5:8-9; Rom. 5:8-9). Theology and doctrine are important, but they are not a substitute for faith and obedience (Jas. 2:18). "Take heed to yourself and to the doctrine. Continue in them, for in doing this you will save both yourself and those who hear you" (1 Tim. 4:16).

CHANGING BELIEFS VERSUS CHANGING BEHAVIOR

The Lord's requirement of repentance prior to salvation (Acts 17:30) should make us realize that Christianity requires more of us than just changing what we believe. Yet some seem slow and even unwilling to change their behavior to the point required by the New Covenant.

James said, "But be doers of the word, and not hearers only, deceiving yourselves. For if anyone is a hearer of the word and not a doer, he is like a man observing his natural face in a mirror; for he observes himself, goes away, and immediately forgets what kind of man he was" (Jas. 1:22-24). While not discounting the importance of attending worship (Heb. 10:24-25), it is not enough to show up every week and listen; we must actually apply the lessons given in God's Word to our lives or we are making a mockery out of Christianity, even if we remain totally oblivious to our own failures. When teaching someone how to preach it is often a good practice to make a video recording so that the flaws are more easily detectable by the person who gives the lesson. That same principle is true with all of Christianity. When we examine God's Word for the type of behavior God expects from his people, we must contrast this with how we conduct our lives in general and then make the necessary modifications.

Some act like God is going to give a written test over the Bible at Judgment Day, instead of realizing that how we live for Him daily IS the test (Col. 2:6-7). "But he who looks into the perfect law of liberty and continues in it, and is not a forgetful hearer but a doer of the work, this one will be blessed in what he does" (Jas. 1:25).

ACCEPTING CRITICISM AND CORRECTION

No one likes to be criticized. Even if we know full well that we are wrong, somehow enduring that correction from someone else is hard to take. But why? Are we not better off when we learn we are wrong and can make the appropriate correction than to remain ignorant of our error and so perpetuate wrong thinking? We might all see this and accept it if it were not for our pride. The wise man said, "Pride goes before destruction, And a haughty spirit before a fall" (Prov. 16:18). Ignorance makes us wrong; pride keeps us wrong.

God had corrected Peter's ignorance about the Gentiles through a vision prior to his conversation with Cornelius (Acts 10:9-20), but Paul later had to remind him of that lesson by criticizing and correcting his behavior (Gal. 2:11-12). He took it well, learned, and changed, as is evidenced by his later referring to "our beloved brother Paul" (2 Pet. 3:15). Peter had learned to accept criticism and grow from it. Apollos was an eloquent man who had a wonderful knowledge of the Old Testament, yet he was ignorant of Jesus. Aquila and Priscilla had to correct him. His acceptance of that correction made him a mighty preacher of the gospel (Acts 18:24-28).

Nitpicking personal criticisms of a person's looks, dress, or mannerisms are uncalled for and uncaring. But biblical criticism and correction is necessary and loving because it addresses a spiritual belief and/or behavior rather than physical attributes or idiosyncrasies. We must learn to forbear the eccentricities of personality and learn to accept criticism and correction when it addresses a spiritual concern. Most of all, we must learn the difference.

DEVELOPING DISCIPLINE

Discipline has received a fairly negative reception in recent years. And since the declining use of corporal punishment in the public classroom has produced such fantastic results (I hope you hear the sarcasm here), we have become a society that now limits our concept of discipline to a test as to whether parents can count to three—not knowing what they might do should they ever get there. This has also led to a church where fewer and fewer people demonstrate self-discipline and where fewer and fewer congregations practice church discipline, yet both of these are fundamental to the spiritual success of the Christian and the congregation.

A Christian must learn to apply lessons from God's Word as directly as possible to every aspect of his life. It is only through this diligent effort that a person can eliminate sinful attitudes and behavior before they become obvious to others. It requires self-control (Gal. 5:23; 2 Pet. 1:6) that ultimately has placed God in control (Gal. 2:20). Self-discipline recognizes personal faults because it looks for them regularly, humbly accepting the reality of weaknesses and addressing them appropriately. The apostle Paul himself wrote, "But I discipline my body and bring it into subjection, lest, when I have preached to others, I myself should become disqualified" (1 Cor. 9:27).

Sometimes, however, self-discipline fails, and that is when we need our brothers and sisters in Christ to step in and help, first through loving correction and instruction (Jas. 5:19-20), then, if necessary, with stern admonition (1 Th. 5:14). If this fails to sway us, then the whole church may need to get involved in order to convince us biblically of our need to repent (Mt. 18:15-20; 2 Th. 3:6). This type of discipline grows out of love for one another and our desire to be close for the right reasons, God's reasons.

Self-discipline is not an exercise in false humility where we seek to disguise our pet sins. Church discipline is not shunning or putting other people down. Discipline is the means by which we train ourselves to keep our behavior in harmony with God's character and help one another stay in the light of God's truth (1 Jn. 1:5-7).

IF YOU DON'T APPLY IT, YOU DON'T REALLY BELIEVE IT

James addressed a significant problem among Jewish Christians early on in the life of the church when the people failed to care for those in need as they should. As he opened his remarks on the subject he said, "What does it profit, my brethren, if someone says he has faith but does not have works? Can faith save him?" (Jas. 2:14). This is an enduring problem for some people whose mouths state firm conviction of the truth but whose behavior is often more like the world. What does their belief profit them? It doesn't. In fact, as James points out, their failure to act in accordance with their stated belief argues that they do not really believe it. "But someone will say, "You have faith, and I have works." Show me your faith without your works, and I will show you my faith by my works" (Jas. 2:18).

Too many Christians behave as if believing all the right things is enough. According to James, such a faith is dead and worthless (Jas. 2:17, 20, 26). It does no good to claim you believe in God and believe the Bible if you do not do what God tells you in the Bible. Yet this attitude runs rampant in many quarters. If you believe God condemns foul language, then you will not use foul language. If you understand that fornication and lasciviousness will keep you out of heaven, you will not commit fornication or participate in lascivious behavior.

The problem is that we do not differentiate between casual belief and faithful conviction. True faith is active belief rather than passive acceptance. Active belief leads directly to obedient action, and nothing less will please God. "You see then that a man is justified by works, and not by faith only" (Jas. 2:24). If you don't apply it, you don't really believe it.

DISCUSSION QUESTIONS:

1. Does our behavior really matter? Give at least three examples of situations where your behavior would/could make a difference to others.

2. What problems could arise for a person who only sees Christianity as a theoretical religion? What are some scriptures this person is rejecting in the process?

3. How is a Christian "tested" over the material in God's word?

4. Some people are hyper-sensitive when it comes to criticism. Others seem to require a smack upside the head to make them realize that correction is warranted. Where do you fall on the "criticism sensitivity spectrum"?

5. What are some potential problems for a touchy, easily upset Christian? Do unruffled, laid-back Christians have an advantage over others, or do they face their own set of challenges?

6. Our God commands the proper types of criticism, correction, and discipline (Gal. 6:1-2; James 5:19-20; 1 Thess. 5:14; Matt. 18:15-20; 2 Thess. 3:6; Eph. 4:15). Why do so many Christians still have trouble accepting and practicing this?

7. When it comes to criticism and correction, what things are OK to tolerate? What things cannot be allowed to "slide"?

8. How is church discipline supposed to work? What are some scriptures that govern the way correction should be handled among brethren?

9. What shows that a person has true faith (belief)?

10. Think about some of the things you have heard/learned in Bible classes, sermons, and your personal study. Do you find it difficult to apply these lessons to your own life? Either way, why do you think this is the case?

ASSIGNMENT:

The lesson mentioned that we should desire to be close to our brethren *"for the right reasons,* God's reasons."

This week make a list of people in the congregation you want to know better and try to set up a time to get together socially, such as for a meal after an assembly.

CHAPTER ELEVEN: GAINING KNOWLEDGE, GROWING FAITH

Young Christians, fresh from the joys of their newfound salvation, sometimes have difficulty understanding and accepting the need to push ever onward in their quest to please God. Paul told the Thessalonians, "Finally then, brethren, we urge and exhort in the Lord Jesus that you should abound more and more, just as you received from us how you ought to walk and to please God" (1 Th. 4:1). The comfort brought by the realization of redemption can quickly turn into complacency if we forget why we obeyed the gospel in the first place. Therefore, we must commit ourselves to building upon the foundation of our salvation a strong relationship with the One who saved us.

Peter referred to the necessity of personal motivation when he told Christians, "as newborn babes, desire the pure milk of the word, that you may grow thereby" (1 Pet. 2:2). We should crave biblical instruction and study so that our understanding of God, the church, and our responsibilities grow and so that, as a result, our faith might grow as well (Rom. 10:17).

Growing as a Christian requires a person to adopt new attitudes, learn new skills, and adjust personal behavior. The foundation for all of these is gaining a thorough understanding of God's revealed will. Once we accept that God knows best and learn what God wants, it should not be hard for us to begin implementing those things necessary to grow. Therefore, we should listen closely to Peter when he writes, "but grow in the grace and knowledge of our Lord and Savior Jesus Christ. To Him be the glory both now and forever. Amen" (2 Pet. 3:18).

LEARNING TO LISTEN

In the first chapter of James, God's servant addressed Christians who blamed God for temptation and their subsequent failures to overcome it. In response to this error James reminded them that God only gives good gifts (Jas. 1:17), and that one example of this is the Word He gave so that we could understand His will (Jas. 1:18), concluding that by making God's Word the model for life we can be saved (Jas. 1:21). Between verses eighteen and twenty-one sits a familiar admonition that rarely receives treatment in its context. James told his readers to "be swift to hear, slow to speak, slow to wrath; for the wrath of man does not produce the righteousness of God" (Jas. 1:19b-20). His point? God has provided the answer for overcoming temptation and understanding life properly within His Word, but it will do us no good if we do not listen to it.

Jesus said, "Therefore, take heed how you hear" (Lk. 8:18a). It is not enough to sit through some sermons and classes. This, by itself, is not really listening. We must open ourselves up to absorb God's Word and the practical applications that stem from it (Jas. 1:22). The Bereans were noble because they listened with purpose (Acts 17:11). They did not listen blindly, but they were listening to learn. Some people's listening skills are designed after the rapid reply model of people who listen just enough to respond but never listen long enough to realize how much they do not know.

Some Christians take pride in their ability to avoid letting the word of God affect them greatly. This is foolish and prideful (Prov. 16:18). A Christian must be ready to listen to what comes from God's word—ready to apply it, ready to relay it, ready to live it. But this will never happen if a Christian is not willing to listen. Paul contrasted Timothy's attitude toward the scriptures (2 Tim. 3:15) with the attitude of some whom Paul said he would find "in the pew" (2 Tim. 4:3-4). Timothy learned because he listened. There is no other way (Rom. 10:17).

LEARNING TO STUDY

Studying the Bible often produces an interesting spectrum of attitudes from people. Some insist they need no assistance in learning God's truth while others believe they cannot learn to study regardless of any assistance they might receive. The eunuch was both willing to accept assistance from Philip and apparently able to think through the process well enough to comprehend it well (Acts 8:30-39). What every Christian must remember is that he has individual responsibility for his knowledge of God's Word and how he applies it (2 Cor. 5:10). You will not be judged based upon the preacher's knowledge or ignorance but by your own.

Learning to study takes extensive and extended effort. In the King James version the word "study" used in 2 Timothy 2:15 refers to the diligence required to make proper ethical decisions based upon God's Word. Therefore, we should never assume that learning God's will is simple; it is, however, worth the effort. Learning to study requires systematic attention directed toward God's Word (1 Tim. 4:13), meditation on and application of the lessons found therein (1 Tim. 4:15), and consistent integration of the lessons learned into everyday life in a visible and sincere way (1 Tim. 4:16; Ps. 119:11).

Most of all, if you are to learn how to study you must first be willing to admit how much you do not know. This is often the first hurdle for many Christians, and one that some struggle with all their lives. The longer you assume any sense of superiority—whether in regard to previous knowledge or personal intelligence—the longer it will take you to learn how to study God's Word properly.

LEARNING TO DISCERN

Young Christians often have such great enthusiasm for everything about the Bible that the devil uses their naïveté to cause them to stumble just as they are beginning their Christian walk (Rom. 6:4). Satan knows how to throw in just enough Bible and just enough "right" to confuse those who remain unprepared for such subtle tactics. But we are not ignorant of his devices (2 Cor. 2:11); therefore, we must learn to discern right from wrong, truth from error, from the very beginning, so that our zeal is directed with proper knowledge (Rom. 10:2).

Christians must learn to put everything people say through a stringent test to make sure that it agrees with what the Bible says (1 Jn. 4:1). After all, it is not that hard to have an opinion. What is difficult is making sure that your beliefs match God's Word (Rom. 10:17). Moreover, we should be proactive in this endeavor. We must "test all things" (1 Th. 5:21) so that we have confidence that we are participating only in what pleases God. Furthermore, we should recognize that we have responsibilities to determine what is best for people rather than just giving them whatever they want (Phil. 1:9-11). We must learn to recognize that even among those who preach there are those whose motives leave something to be desired (Phil. 1:12-18); therefore, we must make sure that our faith is firmly focused on Jesus Christ rather than on any man (1 Cor. 1:10-13).

Discernment requires knowledge of God's will, an understanding of the subtleties of Satan, attention to detail, and practice in exposing hidden agendas. While you should never assume the worst about anyone, you also must never let your guard down to allow Satan to use others to confuse you, tempt you, and destroy you (1 Pet. 5:8).

LEARNING TO FOLLOW

As a general rule, few people really enjoy following someone else. We have all sorts of pithy sayings to back that up. It is amazing that anyone wants to "play second fiddle" considering the way that term is passed around. But not everyone can be "the lead dog." If there is to be any successful effort in which more than one person participates, someone is going to have to take the lead, which also implies that everyone else must be willing to follow. But being a good follower is more difficult than some might think. You must trust your leader enough to put your training in his hands and go where he leads you despite possible conflict and danger.

Christians have the ultimate leader in Jesus Christ. Paul said, "Imitate me, just as I also imitate Christ" (1 Cor. 11:1). The only One that deserves a true "following" in religion is Jesus Christ—not the preacher, not your parents, and not even the apostle Paul should have a following. Learning to follow as a Christian means learning to follow Christ: to accept His leadership, to obey His precepts, and to imitate His example. It is one thing to take the initial steps toward Christ to become a Christian, but following Him means that we are willing to go as far as He requires (Mt. 16:24).

A good follower does not complain, make excuses, or lag behind; a good follower follows. But a good follower also knows whom to follow (Mt. 15:14). Peter wrote, "For to this you were called, because Christ also suffered for us, leaving us an example, that you should follow His steps" (1 Pet. 2:21). Since we do not know the proper way to go in life (Prov. 16:25) and Christ does (Jn. 14:6), we have every reason to follow Him. When we understand that heaven is where we want to go and admit that we do not know how to get there, then it makes perfect sense to commit ourselves to following the One who has already made that journey (Col. 3:1-2).

LEARNING TO LEAD

Many people want to be in the lead, but not very many truly desire the responsibility of leadership. However, all Christians should lead to some degree. But it is something that is learned. Mark records Jesus's original selection of the apostles as a call to learn about leading. "And as He walked by the Sea of Galilee, He saw Simon and Andrew his brother casting a net into the sea; for they were fishermen. Then Jesus said to them, 'Follow Me, and I will make you become fishers of men.' They immediately left their nets and followed Him. When He had gone a little farther from there, He saw James the son of Zebedee, and John his brother, who also were in the boat mending their nets. And immediately He called them, and they left their father Zebedee in the boat with the hired servants, and went after Him" (Mk. 1:16-20).

In order to lead we must first become good followers. We must be willing to sacrifice one way of life for another and change our priorities so that leading takes a more active role. Andrew had already led Peter to Christ prior to this, but together they would learn to lead on a grander scale. As we then review the training of the apostles, we must recognize the centrality of their own spiritual growth as the essential element in spiritual leadership. They needed to mature spiritually if they were to assist others spiritually. They had to travel the road before they could become guides for the journey.

As Peter discovered in a very difficult lesson following his denial of Jesus, learning to lead means learning to love others, learning to teach others, and learning to sacrifice for others. Yet the core of spiritual leadership remains a commitment to follow Jesus Christ (Jn. 21:15-22).

THE GROWTH OF CHARACTER

While we often speak of spiritual growth, growing in knowledge, and growing in faith, it seems we do not speak often enough about what all of this is trying to accomplish: growth in character. But when we consider that the gospel calls on us not only to change our behavior but also to change our thought patterns at the root of our behavior (1 Pet. 1:16; Mt. 5:48; Jn. 13:34-35; 1 Jn. 3:7), we should quickly realize that this implies more than the adoption of different policies or personal directives but a complete positive change in our character.

In order to become a Christian you must first be teachable (Rom. 10:17), but this attitude of openness to the wisdom, experience, and knowledge of others should not end at your conversion. It should go with you throughout life as part of your character. Likewise, we learned about the salvation we gained through our obedience and baptism (Heb. 5:8-9; Acts 2:38) through the message of salvation (Rom. 1:16); therefore, we should press onward in our studies so that our understanding of God's Word increases daily (1 Pet. 2:2). But it is not enough to know the basics of God's Word if we do not develop the wisdom to be able to apply it and to discern when others are abusing it (Jas. 1:22; 2 Pet. 2:1-3). We grow in character when faith fills our lives (Rev. 2:10). This is not a generic verbalization of our beliefs but a conscious effort to incorporate God's will into every aspect of our lives (2 Cor. 5:7). Our character should grow in strength enough to be forward about our faith in such a way as to help others gain the faith they need (1 Cor. 11:1).

A Christian's character should grow throughout his life, regularly applying lessons learned to the realities of life. But maturity is reached only when Christianity becomes his life (Gal. 2:20).

DISCUSSION QUESTIONS:

1. When I was in school, one of my educators tried to teach the students to live by the following phrase: "Know what is right, and do it." How does this apply to Christian growth?

2. Why do so many people—even Christians—blame God when they encounter troubles? According to the first chapter of James, are they justified in doing this?

3. What is the difference between being "a forgetful hearer" (James 1:25) and a good listener (Acts 17:11)?

4. How do you know how much you don't know yet?

5. What is a proper definition of biblical "study" (2 Tim. 2:15)? How does this differ from reading? From mere attentiveness?

6. Discernment is all about making proper evaluations and possessing good judgment. Can this be developed without a thorough understanding of God's word? Why or why not?

7. In seeking to develop discernment, how does one balance the effort to gain an understanding of the way Satan operates (2 Cor. 2:11) without becoming jaded and cynical?

8. What makes it difficult to be a good follower?

9. What is so difficult about being a good leader?

10. We ought to be growing in spiritual character. What is character? How does one determine that a characteristic is "spiritual"?

ASSIGNMENT:

Read Galatians 2:20. How is one "crucified with Christ"? How does Christ "live in you"? What would this say about the maturity level of a Christian brother or sister?

This week, identify two things about your life that need to change in order to better reflect Christ. Begin working on them immediately and ask for help from mature Christians as you work at growing in these areas. Come prepared to discuss the challenges you face in making these changes and growing for Christ.

CHAPTER TWELVE:
THE CHALLENGES THAT LIE AHEAD

Avoiding any mention of the inevitable challenges a Christian will face in life may postpone when a young disciple has to face that reality, but it also leaves him completely unprepared for that reality. Jesus told His disciples about the challenges they would face in their future on the very night of His betrayal, and it is this model that we should emulate.

Jesus warned His disciples that they would likely face depression due to His physical departure (Jn. 14:1, 27), but that the gospel message inspired by the Holy Spirit would fill that teaching void (Jn. 14:26). He spoke to them about the great responsibility they had (Jn. 15:15-16, 26-27), and of the persecution they would face (Jn. 15:18-16:4). He told them all of this specifically so that they "should not be made to stumble" (Jn. 16:1) but would rather have their faith strengthened as a result (Jn. 16:4). You do not help others by denying challenges exist; you help them by preparing them for the challenges that you are sure exist.

At the core of Jesus's own preparation of His disciples was the challenge of the cross that was before Him in the next few hours (Jn. 16:19-24). And despite the knowledge that His own disciples would desert Him during His greatest challenge, He took comfort in knowing He would please the Father and would ultimately be victorious (Jn. 16:32-33). At this time of ultimate challenge, Jesus prayed (Jn. 17:1-26). All Christians will face challenges in their lives spiritually. What we must do is take up the challenge now to prepare for the challenges that will come our way.

THERE'S ALWAYS MORE TO LEARN

The apostle Paul had an enviable education for someone who would spend his life addressing the errors of Judaizing teaching while spreading the gospel. He had been "brought up . . . at the feet of Gamaliel, taught according to the strictness of our fathers' law, and was zealous toward God...." (Acts 22:3) and had received direct revelation from Jesus Christ (Gal. 1:12). Yet at the end of his life, after years of faithful service, study, and preaching, he wrote to Timothy, "Bring the cloak that I left with Carpus at Troas when you come—and the books, especially the parchments" (2 Tim. 4:13). While it is impossible to detect the exact identity of these books and parchments, the urgency with which Paul wrote shows how much he valued them personally. If the much-studied apostle Paul realized the value of continuing education even at the end of his life, then surely we can deduce from this that there is always more to learn when it comes to our spiritual education.

While a young Christian usually realizes how much there is to learn, once that material has been learned it is easy to become apathetic toward spiritual education. One of the saddest sights in any congregation is to see older Christians who have stopped learning and stopped growing spiritually. But surely this did not happen by deliberate choice! Somewhere along the line they became content with their present level of knowledge and plateaued.

Once a young Christian has found the beauty of the truth, he should commit himself to unearthing scriptural treasures for the remainder of his life. If we evaluate our understanding by a checklist of doctrines, we will always come up short. If we keep the Word of God in the forefront, we will always remember how much more there is yet to learn (1 Pet. 2:2).

SPIRITUAL GROWTH

Most Christians understand that, at least in theory, they are to grow spiritually. But many of them do not know what that means. For many, spiritual growth is equated with an understanding of the Bible. But while a growing understanding of the Bible is necessary for spiritual growth, they are not the same thing. In his second epistle, Peter closed by saying, "but grow in the grace and knowledge of our Lord and Savior Jesus Christ" (2 Pet. 3:18a). Spiritual growth requires that we grow in two separate components: grace and knowledge. They are related, but distinct. And in order to grow spiritually we need both to understand and implement them together.

Growing in knowledge requires a commitment to diligent investigation of truth (2 Tim. 2:15). Growing in grace (favor) requires a deep thankfulness for the very opportunity to enjoy such a relationship with God and a commitment to applying those things we learn so that we might please God and enjoy His favor more and more (1 Th. 4:1; Jn. 17:17). Spiritual growth does not occur until both of these aspects are present consistently.

Growing spiritual knowledge is essential because you must know what you should do before you can do it. But at the same time, if you understand the Bible theoretically but remain unaffected in the way you think and therefore in how you live your life, how has your study profited you? Someone can know every word of the Bible by heart and yet be a miserable person because the message has not truly entered the heart. Spiritual growth is therefore judged not by how much you know but by how well you live. "I have been crucified with Christ; it is no longer I who live, but Christ lives in me; and the *life* which I now live in the flesh I live by faith in the Son of God, who loved me and gave Himself for me" (Gal. 2:20).

PLANNING FOR ETERNITY

We live in a society dominated by the "now." We want faster computers, faster service, and faster food. If something is important we want it done yesterday. Our society caters to our wants and puts off dealing with our needs. We are a debtor society because we want more than what we have while ignoring what we actually need. As a result, we spend most of our time worrying about immediate wants and little time preparing for what lies ahead. The future will just have to wait. But all of this should change when we become Christians, because we must change from thinking in terms of time to thinking in terms of eternity.

The apostle John reminds us, "And this is the promise that he has promised us--eternal life" (1 Jn. 2:25). Furthermore, Paul said that he lived "in hope of eternal life which God, who cannot lie, promised before time began" (Tit. 1:2). For a child of God with true faith (2 Cor. 5:7), eternal life is as real as anything currently in existence. A Christian lives not for the moment but for that moment when He meets His Savior face to face (1 Jn. 3:2).

If we think temporally (time-based), we will be satisfied with a temporal existence and a temporal reward. It is only when we think in terms of eternity that we will live for an eternal existence with an eternal reward. Paul explained his own motivation for living and preaching to the Corinthians. "Therefore we do not lose heart. Even though our outward man is perishing, yet the inward man is being renewed day by day. For our light affliction, which is but for a moment, is working for us a far more exceeding and eternal weight of glory, while we do not look at the things which are seen, but at the things which are not seen. For the things which are seen are temporary, but the things which are not seen are eternal" (2 Cor. 4:16-18).

BECOMING A LEADER BEGINS NOW

Every congregation of the Lord's people needs leadership. Sadly, only a relatively small number of congregations have true leadership—leadership that goes beyond a title and basic decision making to visionary thinking built around a knowledge of and dedication to the scriptures. This situation exists because few seem to understand the importance of a lifelong training process in becoming a spiritual leader.

All Christians should become well acquainted with the qualifications for elders (Tit. 1:5-9; 1 Tim. 3:1-7), deacons (1 Tim. 3:8-13), preachers (1 Tim. 4:12-16), worship leaders (1 Tim. 2:1-12), and teachers (Jas. 3:1, 17). While some note that most of the qualities mentioned should be true for all Christians, the point they should understand is that these qualities must exist in that person's life before they are qualified to take on that role. Therefore, until a person has demonstrated the development of his own character as prescribed by God's Word, he has no business leading others in the spiritual realm. Developing maturity in these areas takes time and dedication; therefore, it is essential that Christians begin immediately if they are to achieve the growth necessary for the responsibilities of leadership.

Spiritual leadership does not come by appointment. Rather the appointment should come in recognition of the prior existence of spiritual leadership. A congregation that accepts politicking for leadership positions will get politicians for their leaders—in the worst sense of that word. But many congregations go ahead with this because the members have not prepared themselves for anything better. The church will need solid, spiritual leaders in the future, which is why young Christians need to begin preparing themselves today.

DISCUSSION QUESTIONS:

1. In John 14-17, what types of challenges did Jesus warn His disciples about? Have you faced any of those challenges yet as a Christian? If so, how do you think you are handling them so far?

2. Once a Christian has washed away his or her sins at baptism, what is so important about continuing to prepare for spiritual challenges?

3. To you, which is sadder: an older Christian who has ceased to learn and grow or a young Christian who quickly loses his zeal for the Lord? Why are both so damaging to the Lord's church?

4. "Spiritual growth requires that we grow in two separate components: grace and knowledge." Can you give specific examples of both?

5. What is the true standard of spiritual growth? How do you know when you are spiritually mature?

6. As a Christian, should you think more in terms of time or in terms of eternity? Which is more natural to do in our society?

7. Does eternity seem real to you? Why or why not?

8. Why is true spiritual leadership such a challenge, even for those who have been Christians for many years? Why is it important to be a "visionary thinker" as a leader?

9. How do you know when a person is qualified to be a spiritual leader?

10. Why is it so important to begin preparing for spiritual leadership now (if you haven't already begun)?

ASSIGNMENT:

What types of spiritual leadership do you intend to become qualified for as you mature in your Christianity? Please give specific examples of the things you will need to do to become capable of fulfilling those responsibilities.

CHAPTER THIRTEEN:
WHAT KIND OF CHRISTIAN WILL YOU BE?

Once you become a Christian, you awaken to all kinds of new responsibilities and all sorts of new possibilities. You are giving up your former life to create a new and better one (Col. 3:5-11). Of course, it will only become a better life if you pursue that course with perseverance. But, most of all, you must decide from the beginning to overcome the temptation to fall back into old habits and instead rise to the heights that God has made available.

You ultimately determine the type of Christian you will be. And, believe it or not, how you begin as a Christian has a great effect on what you eventually become. If you become active in the work of the church today, you are more likely to be active years from now (1 Cor. 15:58). If you fight against temptation now, you train yourself to do so for a lifetime (Jas. 1:12). If you learn how to live and live to learn (Psa. 119:11, 97, 105), you will have provided the background for lasting spiritual growth (1 Pet. 2:2; 2 Pet. 3:18). On the other hand, if you view your immersion into Christ as the final step in the process rather than the first step forward in a new existence (Rom. 6:3-4), then you will likely regress spiritually rather than make progress.

No one plans to be a spiritual failure. It happens due to neglect, inattention, lack of concentration, and low expectations. Therefore, we must begin our new lives in Christ with a zeal that comes from a full realization of what we have gained rather than just the emotion of the moment. We must set our course on heaven and not look back (Phil. 3:13-14). We must look to the scriptures to see what God expects of us with confidence that we can become what He says we can become. When we make these changes within, we have begun the process to give lifelong meaning to the word "conversion."

A BABY CHRISTIAN

When you originally obey the gospel, you become a babe in Christ, a descriptive term stemming from the new birth of baptism (Jn. 3:3-5) and a person's relative spiritual age. Therefore, every Christian was, at some point, a babe. We all had to start learning and growing in Christ at this new beginning, regardless of our previous knowledge. However, no Christian should be content with spiritual "baby" status. It is not wrong to be young in the faith, but it can be deadly to remain so indefinitely.

Writing to the Corinthians, the apostle Paul said, "And I, brethren, could not speak to you as to spiritual people but as to carnal, as to babes in Christ. I fed you with milk and not with solid food; for until now you were not able to receive it, and even now you are still not able; for you are still carnal. For where there are envy, strife, and divisions among you, are you not carnal and behaving like mere men?" (1 Cor. 3:1-3). Paul had expected the Corinthians to grow spiritually, yet the nature of their problems—indicative of their stunted growth in character—exposed their ongoing spiritual infancy. Paul rebuked the Corinthians for their inability or refusal to grow up, spiritually speaking.

While a young Christian is still a babe in Christ, other Christians can patiently forbear and instruct him in various matters that he has yet to realize matter to God. However, every Christian must eventually develop the knowledge and character to do these things for himself, just as a baby must learn to walk, eat, and care for himself rather than forever remain dependent upon his parents. A baby Christian fails to learn what his new life is all about and returns to the familiar dependency of spiritual ignorance and sinful slavery. Few people aspire to this when they obey the gospel, but they still fall victim to it because they do not aspire to anything better (Heb. 5:12-6:3).

A WEAK CHRISTIAN

Weakness rarely receives praise, regardless of the sphere in which that weakness exists. In athletics, your opponent will study you to determine your weaknesses. The same could be said in a chess tournament. In other cases, weakness might refer to an illness that has left a person without strength. Regardless of the sphere, weakness implies vulnerability to attack. Therefore, we should consider this underlying theme when we read Paul's exhortation telling us to "uphold the weak" (1 Th. 5:14). Christians have a ruthless enemy in Satan (1 Pet. 5:8), and like a lion stalking an antelope, the devil preys on weakness.

Weak Christians are those people who constantly require assistance and attention in spiritual matters in order to keep them from completely abandoning their Lord. They have had problems letting go of the life they led prior to their conversion (Col. 3:5-11), and after months and even years of opportunities to learn, they still have difficulty overcoming the same temptations they faced when they first obeyed. They may attend regularly or sporadically, but their weakness limits their involvement in the church because they never really committed to that new way of life.

Weak Christians need support from those who are stronger and more experienced in the faith in order to handle the problems inherent in life. But at some point, those weak Christians have to exercise their faith (Jas. 1:2-4) so that it might grow and stand on their own faith rather than being propped up by others. Weak Christians must move beyond "I know God says that, but..." to making their faith active and strong so that they might one day help others. "But be doers of the word, and not hearers only, deceiving yourselves" (Jas. 1:22).

A DISORDERLY CHRISTIAN

The acceptance of God's standard for our way of life is inherent in the plan of salvation. Since we must first turn to God's Word in realization that He has the only plan that can save (Rom. 10:17), accept it in its totality without amendment (Heb. 11:6; Col. 3:17), agree to make whatever changes are required according to that standard (Acts 17:30), commit ourselves verbally to submitting to Jesus Christ and the authority contained in His Word (Rom. 10:9-10; Jn. 12:48), and pledge our allegiance and obedience to Him (Heb.

5:8-9) through immersion in water (Acts 2:38; 8:36-38), then throughout the process of conversion we should have recognized that we were choosing to submit ourselves to a higher way of life and that we will be held responsible to that commitment.

Unfortunately, some people either did not seriously consider their commitment at the time or have forgotten that commitment over time. As a result, they no longer "walk by the same rule" as instructed in the gospel (Phil 3:16). To be "disorderly" (2 Th. 3:11) or "unruly" (1 Th. 5:14) is to be out of rank and out of order. Christians' lives should show the same commitment to Christian standards. When someone ignores those standards, he sticks out like a soldier who refuses to participate with his unit in forming a straight line. As such, the disorderly Christian is a disruptive force in the army of the Lord who should be warned about the condition of his character and corrected immediately (1 Th. 5:14).

In some cases, a Christian's heart is so hardened that he turns away from the instruction offered from God, regardless of the care exercised by those who attempt to speak with him. In that case, "we command you, brethren, in the name of our Lord Jesus Christ, that you withdraw from every brother who walks disorderly and not according to the tradition which he received from us" (2 Th. 3:6).

A HYPOCRITICAL CHRISTIAN

Despite the many outstanding examples of morality and godliness available to people in the world and to unfaithful Christians, they inevitably refer to "all those hypocrites in the church" in an attempt to excuse their own disobedience. While the number of full-blown hypocrites in the church is highly exaggerated, sadly, they do exist. Sometimes people are unaware of the inconsistencies in their lives. Sometimes younger Christians have yet to learn what changes they should make. But sometimes Christians fail to repent of their sins and allow the world to shape their lives regardless of all they claim about standing by the scriptures.

Jesus noted this same type of behavior among the scribes and Pharisees of His day: "Therefore whatever they tell you to observe, that observe and do, but do not do according to their works; for they say, and do not do" (Matt. 23:3).

Some people truly are all talk. They have a few issues that they emphasize to everyone else, but they neglect the weightier matters (Matt. 23:3). Many times these people should know better, but their attitude prevents any real learning and growing (Mt. 23:2). The scribes and the Pharisees liked to find faults in others, especially on their pet topics (Mt. 23:4), but their greatest flaw was the heart of hypocrisy, because as Jesus said, in "all their works they do to be seen by men" (Matt. 23:5). They wanted the attention given to spiritual men, yet they lacked a spiritual heart (Matt. 23:6-7).

No Christian should knowingly follow the pattern of the scribes and Pharisees. Instead, we should all give the greatest diligence to avoid any hint of such hypocritical behavior. Therefore, we must make doing God's Word as important as hearing it (Jas. 1:22), and we must love pleasing God without regard to the praise of men (Jn. 12:42-43).

A COMPLAINING CHRISTIAN

Complaining often falls into that category of sins that are excused because "that's just so-and-so." However, God does not allow such exceptions. Apparently, many people do not understand the extent of damage caused by the wagging tongues of negative naysayers. The apostle Paul told the Philippians, "Do all things without complaining and disputing, that you may become blameless and harmless, children of God without fault in the midst of a crooked and perverse generation, among whom you shine as lights in the world" (Phil. 2:14-15). According to Paul, if a person was a complainer, he was not blameless, harmless, or without rebuke, nor could he shine as a light to the world.

Complaining is very different from offering a scriptural objection. Complaining means that people have an objection to something—sometimes anything—but that they object for personal reasons rather than biblical reasons. If they had biblical reasons, they would cite scripture and explain their reasons for interpreting scripture differently. Instead, they want to get their way, and they will talk, gossip, nag, argue, and politic until they get their way.

While people, including those in the church, often give in to complainers just to "keep the peace," God never does. Sometimes the squeaky wheel does not need grease at all. Sometimes there is a bunch of gunk getting in the way and keeping the wheel from operating properly. When this is the case, you do not add grease, you get rid of the gunk. Complaining is sinful and will cost you your soul. Therefore, do not "complain, as some of them also complained, and were destroyed by the destroyer" (1 Cor. 10:10).

A WORKING CHRISTIAN

When a coach looks over his roster of athletes, he must make a decision: who is active and who is inactive? An athlete might be declared inactive due to poor health or even because of a bad attitude. But the coach must make such decisions because someone who is effectively inactive will hurt the team if he is unable to perform the tasks assigned to him.

Every Christian has the responsibility to get involved in the work of the church. The nature of our participation may vary due to skill or natural areas of interest, but what should not vary is our commitment to pleasing God (2 Tim. 2:15) and furthering the gospel (Phil. 1:12). Some people will be in the forefront of the work, and others will work behind the scenes. Some will be prominent in evangelism, while others will emphasize edification. Some may take the lead in forming plans and taking action, while others hold up their hands and encourage them in the work undertaken. All of these are important in keeping the work of the church vibrant (Tit. 2:14-15). You do not have to do everything in the church, but every Christian must do something. You cannot go to heaven riding on the coattails of others (Gal. 6:5).

All Christians should be workers in the kingdom, but unfortunately, not every Christian is willing to do so. As a result, everyone else must bear an additional part of the load. When we consider all the effort that the Lord has put forth on our behalf, how sad that some are not willing to participate in the work done for Him. If our Christianity is to have lasting value, it must be active, and if it is active, we must be working. "Therefore, my beloved brethren, be steadfast, immovable, always abounding in the work of the Lord, knowing that your labor is not in vain in the Lord" (1 Cor. 15:58).

A SPIRITUAL CHRISTIAN

After Paul's lengthy discussion regarding what it takes to walk in the Spirit, he addressed an important responsibility Christians have toward one another when we fail. He wrote, "Brethren, if a man is overtaken in any trespass, you who are spiritual restore such a one in a spirit of gentleness, considering yourself lest you also be tempted" (Gal. 6:1). While identifying the person "overtaken in a fault" should not be that difficult, finding Christians who are truly "spiritual" can sometimes be more difficult.

A spiritual Christian is one who turns to the instruction provided by the Holy Spirit for the development of his character and the determination of his behavior. This was Paul's point throughout the previous passage (Gal. 5:16-26). A spiritual person rejects the lusts of the flesh and pursues the fruit of the Spirit. He recognizes that he owes his spiritual life to the gospel and thus continues to build his life spiritually through those inspired words (1 Th. 2:13). But as Paul also demonstrates, a spiritual Christian has greater responsibilities. Because he has grown spiritually himself to recognize sin for what it is, he has the moral obligation to help others learn these lessons through calm confrontation and patient instruction.

A spiritual Christian does not become proud or haughty in his knowledge, because he understands all too well that he remains perpetually at risk of giving in to temptation just as much as anyone else. However, his commitment to spiritual knowledge and spiritual growth make it possible for him to declare to others, "Imitate me, just as I also imitate Christ" (1 Cor. 11:1).

A FAITHFUL CHRISTIAN

Despite the various appellations previously cited, there is really only one kind of Christian that counts with God—a faithful Christian. Jesus told the church in Smyrna, "Do not fear any of those things which you are about to suffer. Indeed, the devil is about to throw some of you into prison, that you may be tested, and you will have tribulation ten days. Be faithful until death, and I will give you the crown of life" (Rev. 2:10). All Christians should strive for complete faithfulness in all that they do, regardless of the consequences involved in this life but completely mindful of the consequences in eternity.

Being faithful means being full of faith. Since "faith comes by hearing, and hearing by the word of God" (Rom. 10:17), then faithfulness depends upon our being filled with the word of God (Jas. 1:21). This is not simply a matter of rote memorization or doctrinal recitation. Being filled with the word of

God means that it encompasses every aspect of our lives (Col. 3:16-17) so that God's word guides our decisions as we walk along life's pathway (2 Cor. 5:7). A faithful Christian does not ponder whether or not to accept what God says; a faithful Christian diligently studies God's word and then accepts its message completely (Acts 17:11). A faithful Christian has grown beyond infancy, has overcome weakness, marches in step with the Lord, strives for complete honesty, openness, and consistency in life, does not complain, works diligently in the kingdom, and contemplates all matters, including the needs of others, from a spiritual point of view.

The faithful Christian is the one to whom the Lord promised to say, "Well done, good and faithful servant; you were faithful over a few things, I will make you ruler over many things. Enter into the joy of your lord" (Matt. 25:21).

QUESTIONS:

1. "How you begin as a Christian has a great effect on what you eventually become." Why is this true?

2. God believes that we can all be faithful, active Christians (Rev. 2:10; 1 Cor. 15:57-58). How do we gain the necessary confidence to make this a reality?

3. We all know people who have always been like "Peter Pan"—they never really grew up. Why is it dangerous to do this spiritually?

4. Our adversary, the devil, is like a roaring lion (1 Peter 5:8). Lions are known for preying on the weak or injured animals of a herd. Does this mean that the devil only goes after "weak" Christians?

5. All Christians have weaknesses, so what makes someone a weak Christian?

6. What happens to disorderly soldiers in an army? Why are disorderly Christians such a danger to the Lord's army (2 Thess. 3:11)?

7. What are the differences between a weak Christian and a disorderly Christian (1 Thess. 5:14)?

8. Is complaining really that big a deal? Why or why not?

9. Read 1 Corinthians 12:12-31. What applications can you make from this

passage about working Christians?

10. One hears about famous people who are considered to be "really spiritual" by their peers (even if they have nothing to do with "organized religion"). This usually means that they are committed to some form of morality, that they are "true to themselves," or that they seem to be in harmony with nature. What really makes a person "spiritual" according to God's way of thinking?

ASSIGNMENT:

Study the parable of the talents from Matthew 25:14-30. Our goal should be to live as faithful Christian servants. From this lesson, what biblical principles can you gather to help you know if you're actually faithful?

While this ends our study, the point of Christ's parable is that what you do from this point forward will determine your faithfulness and therefore your eternity. Therefore, the final assignment is a simple one given originally by Jesus Himself: "Be faithful until death, and I will give you the crown of life" (Rev. 2:10c).

OTHER TITLES FROM HOPKINS PUBLISHING

BUILDING BLOCKS

In this heftier sequel to Beyond Baptism, Kevin W. Rhodes walks readers through thirteen topics necessary to ground Christians in the faith and correct common misunderstandings.

No Apologies

Kevin Cauley provides the Lord's church with a useful resource in the field of Christian Evidences by presenting the case for Christian faith in a manner that is both thorough and understandable.

THE GLAM GIRL'S GUIDE TO SEX

This straight forward study breaks down what a girl is going through as she matures and offers biblical guidance as she contemplates decisions that affect her opinions, actions and most importantly the destination of her soul.

SINGLED OUT

An enriching study for young women designed to help you find identity and contentment in your relationship with God whether or not you have found a spouse.

A Series of 52 Bible Lessons

J.W. McGarvey provides an excellent resource: one full year of curriculum for the Bible class program or home devotional studies for the serious Bible Student.

TO KNOW THE LOVE OF CHRIST

A series of Bible studies which teach the fundamentals of New Testament Christianity They can be used as an evangelistic tool, or as a personal course of study.

ANNUAL SOUTHWEST BIBLE LECTURES

Contains two quarters of material for Bible class curriculum, with concise lessons and thought provoking questions.

Books from previous years are also available!

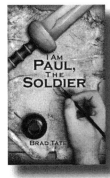

I AM PAUL, THE SOLDIER

"Paul, a soldier of the cross, endured ups and downs and is awaiting his eternal reward. This book will encourage you to be faithful in your ups and down in order to receive eternal life."

SPEAKING FROM THE HEART

This is a one year devotional guide, written by members of the Karns Church of Christ in Knoxville, TN. The articles are intended to uplift our spirits and challenge our attitudes and actions to be more closely conformed to the image of Jesus.

MY BOOK OF WORSHIP NOTES

This book of note pages provides space to take notes in worship for one solid year. Now your kids can listen to the sermon, take notes, write down scripture references, and draw a personal application of the lesson.

THE BEST PLACE TO LAY AN EGG

In a lively and whimsical way, Emily Hopkins takes you into the minds of a bunch of hens...

Dash The Racecar

Come join Dash as he commits to the race of a lifetime, and see how you can get the greatest prize of all... eternity with Jesus!!!

Johnny Had A Dollar

Johnny has a dollar. Now the question is what to do with it? As this young boy considers all the many things he could do, he tries to decide what would be best.

ALPHABEAR

From the author of Johnny Had A Dollar, comes a delightful way to teach young children how to alphabetize.

Made in the USA
San Bernardino,
CA